PENGUIN BOOKS

UNDER THE DUVET

Marian Keyes lives in Dublin with her husband. She has written five novels: *Watermelon*, *Lucy Sullivan is Getting Married*, *Rachel's Holiday*, *Last Chance Saloon* and *Sushi for Beginners*, all of them international bestsellers.

Marian Keyes

Under the Duvet

Notes on High Heels, Movie Deals, Wagon Wheels, Shoes,
Reviews, Having the Blues, Builders, Babies,
Families and Other Calamities

PENGUIN BOOKS

PENGUIN BOOKS

Published by the Penguin Group
Penguin Books Ltd, 80 Strand, London WC2R ORL, England
Penguin Putnam Inc., 375 Hudson Street, New York, New York 10014, USA
Penguin Books Australia Ltd, 250 Camberwell Road, Camberwell,
Victoria 3124, Australia
Penguin Books Canada Ltd, 10 Alcorn Avenue, Toronto, Ontario, Canada M4V 3B2
Penguin Books India (P) Ltd, 11 Community Centre, Panchsheel Park,
New Delhi – 110 017, India
Penguin Books (NZ) Ltd, Cnr Rosedale and Airborne Roads,
Albany, Auckland, New Zealand
Penguin Books (South Africa) (Pty) Ltd, 24 Sturdee Avenue,
Rosebank 2196, South Africa

Penguin Books Ltd, Registered Offices: 80 Strand, London WC2R ORL, England

www.penguin.com

First published by Michael Joseph 2001
Published in Penguin Books 2002
1

Set in Monotype Fournier
Printed in England by Clays Ltd, St Ives plc

Contents

Introduction

When I was twenty-one I got it into my head that I wanted to be a journalist. I considered my options: I could buy a pork-pie hat and notebook and approach newspapers, or I could apply to do a course. I decided on the course, which happened to be vastly oversubscribed, but I got through several of the interviewing stages, as they whittled down the numbers. However, I didn't make the final cut and I was absolutely devastated – heartbroken! But with the wisdom of hindsight it was probably all for the best. I would have been a terrible journalist – too wussy to doorstep suspects and too afraid of giving offence to ask tough questions. And I think I misunderstood my desire to work with words: I wanted to write fiction, not fact.

Anyway, years passed (nine of them) and eventually I did begin to write fiction, which is when I discovered a peculiar side-effect of being a novelist: newspaper and magazine editors were keen for me to contribute pieces of – wait for it – *journalism*.

Once I established that I didn't have to dissect burning matters of the day and that it was perfectly OK to write funny autobiographical pieces, I was happy to do so. I began doing a regular monthly column for *Irish Tatler*, which covered most aspects of my life – writing, touring, trying to buy a house and learn to drive, my great love of shoes and confectionery, my great fear of dogs and New Year's Eve. Occasionally other Irish publications commissioned articles on something specific like Mother's Day or summer holidays, and over the months and years, without noticing, I built up quite a hefty pile of journalism.

Most of the articles in this collection have been published already in Ireland, but not all have been. Some others I've incorporated into a novel – like the story of me going for a mud-wrap in a desperate attempt to lose weight two days before I got married. Those of you who've read *Last Chance Saloon* might remember Tara having a similar experience.

Everything in this book really did happen to me, but occasionally I've changed some details and people's names to protect the innocent or not-so-innocent! The majority of the articles are humorous, but a few aren't quite as light-hearted – in particular the piece about struggling with alcoholism. (But you can skip it if it makes you depressed!) That's the beauty of a collection like this – unlike a novel, it can be read in any order you please; you can even start at the back if you want. I like the idea that this is something you can dip in and out of, that you can let the book fall open on a random page and just start reading (unless you've read it already, of course).

Many people were instrumental in this book coming together and I'd like to thank them all; in particular, Tony (aka Himself) for his Trojan work collating the pieces, and

Louise Moore and Harriet Evans for their creative and meticulous editing. Finally, I'd like to thank Ian Davidson for inspiring this collection.

And thank you very much for reading this book. I sincerely hope you enjoy it.

Marian Keyes

OH, THE GLAMOUR

Paperback Writher

When people ask me what I do for a crust and I tell them that I'm a novelist, they immediately assume that my life is a non-stop carousel of limos, television appearances, hair-dos, devoted fans, stalkers and all the glitzy paraphernalia of being a public figure.

It's time to set the record straight.

I write alone, in a darkened bedroom, wearing my PJs, eating bananas, my laptop on a pillow in front of me. Occasionally – it usually coincides with promoting a book – I am led, blinking, into the daylight, and when I try to talk to people, discover that I'm not able to, that I've become completely desocialized. And as for being mobbed by adoring fans – I'm *never* recognized. Once I thought I was, but I was mistaken. I was in a shoeshop (where else?), and when I asked one of the girls if she had any of these sixteen shoes in my size, she looked at me, put her hand on her chest and gave a little gasp. 'It's you!' she declared.

It is, I thought, thrilled to the marrow. It *is* me – I'm famous!

'Yes,' the girl continued. 'You were in the pub last night, you were the one singing, weren't you?'

I was so disappointed I could hardly speak. I'd been nowhere near any pub the night before.

'You've a great voice,' she said. 'Now what size do you want these shoes in?'

Even the day a book comes out isn't as life-altering as I'd once anticipated. The morning my first book *Watermelon* was officially published in England, where I lived at the time, I half-expected that people in the street would look at me differently as I went to work. That they'd nudge each other and mutter, 'See her, that's that Marian Keyes, she's written a book.' And that the bus conductor might let me off my fare. ('You're OK there, Writer-Girl, this one's on me.') But, naturally, no one paid me the slightest attention. At lunchtime I rushed to the nearest bookshop, my heart aflutter, as I expected to see my beloved creation in a massive display. Instead I found the latest John Grisham piled high *where my book should have been*. I looked for a smaller display of my book. None to be seen. Mortified, I went to the shelf and searched alphabetically. And found it wasn't there. So I went to the counter and got the girl to look it up on the computer.

'Oh, that,' she said, eyeing the screen. 'We're not getting any in.'

'I can order you a copy, though,' she called after me, as I slunk away to shoot myself.

For a couple of weeks afterwards, whenever my boss left the office I grabbed the phone and systematically rang every bookshop in London, pretending to be a customer, asking if they stocked *Watermelon*. And if they hadn't got it, I rang again a few days later, hoping they'd changed their minds. In the end, I'm sure they recognized my voice. I imagined them putting their hands over the mouthpiece and shouting, 'It's that Keyes one again. Have we got her bloody book in yet?'

As well as expecting glitz and glamour, I used to think that an integral part of being a writer was lying around on a couch, eating chocolate raisins, waiting for the muse to strike. And that if the muse hadn't struck, I might as well be watching Jerry Springer while I was waiting. So it came as a nasty shock to discover that if I was waiting for the muse to come a-calling, it would take several decades to write a book.

So now, muse or no muse, I work eight hours a day, Monday to Friday, just like I did when I was an accounts clerk. The main difference is that I work in bed. Not because I am a lazy lump (OK, not *just* because I'm a lazy lump), but just because the idea of sitting at a desk daunts me and frankly, I'm daunted enough. So the bed it is and it's worked out nicely so far, especially since I started turning myself regularly to avoid bedsores.

Most days I start work at about eight o'clock – kicking the day off with a good dose of terror. Today is the day, I usually think, when I run out of ideas, when the inspiration packs its bags and goes to find another accounts clerk and transforms their life.

People often ask me where I get my ideas from and, God, I wish I knew. All I can say is that I find people fascinating, and seeing as I write about emotional landscapes, this can only be a good thing. I think that on a subconscious level I'm taking in information constantly, and in case I come across extra-specially interesting people or funny sayings, I carry a notebook with me at all times. Well, actually I don't. I'm *supposed* to, and when I give advice to aspiring writers that's always what I tell them to do. But somehow when I forage around amongst the sweet papers and lip glosses in my hand-bag the notebook is never there. So my 'office' (i.e., the floor on my side of the bed) is littered with bus-tickets and pastille wrappers with little notes to myself scribbled on them.

Another question that I'm often asked is if there's any downside to being a writer. Three words: the crippling insecurity. In my old job, I worked in accounts. It may not have been the most exciting job in the universe, but it was very reassuring. If it balanced I knew I was right – it was as simple as that. But with writing, there's no right or wrong, it's all just a matter of opinion. One of my hardest times as a writer was when my second book came out and someone told me they preferred the first. 'It's not as good,' she complained sulkily, as if I'd done it specifically to spite her.

'Thank you for your comments,' I replied heartily. 'And would you mind passing me that cut-throat razor. I'm off to have a bath.'

And there's more! For example, I tried to get an agent *after* I'd been accepted for publication. Smugly, I assumed it would be no bother, seeing as the hard work of securing a publisher had already been done. Instead I got a snooty letter saying that the agent didn't feel mine was the kind of work she wanted to represent. I was absolutely devastated, and tormented myself during many a sleepless night wondering about these mysterious authors that she *did* want to represent.

It took me a long time to see that this woman's rejection of me was *only one person's opinion*. Which leads me smoothly to my next gripe – bad reviews. The first time someone slagged my book in print I was genuinely baffled by how nasty they were. 'What did I ever do to her?' I wondered aloud and at length, and only stopped when my nearest and dearest begged me to shut up. Five books later, I've got a lot better at dealing with it. A bad review is never a reason to throw my hat in the air and burst into an impromptu version of 'Knees Up, Mother Brown', but nor is it a reason to take to my bed with a box of Miniature Heroes for a day or two either. (I need no excuse to do that.) I've got better at accepting that I can't please everyone. I've also got better at accepting that critics are often happy to review books without going to the trouble of actually reading them: that became clear when one broadsheet described *Rachel's Holiday* – a novel about recovering from drug addiction – as 'forgettable froth'.

Another potential minefield is the possibility of real life leaking into what I write. I love my friends and I'm keen to hold on to them, so if they're going through dramas, tempting though it may be, I have to make sure that not even a hint sneaks into a storyline. Similarly, my characters are entirely made up – amalgams of several characteristics gleaned from dozens, maybe even hundreds, of different people. Hopefully, at some stage in the book they transcend the sum of their parts and become 'real'. But not *real* real, if you know what I mean. All the same, that doesn't stop people seeing either themselves or others re-created as fictional characters. More than once someone has said to me, 'Oh-ho! So-and-so won't be too pleased to see you've stuck her in your book! *And* implied that she's unfaithful to her husband.'

But *apart* from that, Mrs Lincoln, how did you enjoy the play? – Despite the few downsides, I get tremendous pleasure from what I do. And even more pleasure from the fact that other people seem to enjoy it.

Though I'm told it actually happens, I still find it hard to credit that people will part with their hard-earned cash for something that I've created. One of the nicest experiences I've ever had was recently in a bookshop. They had a lovely display of my books, which gave me a great buzz, especially because I'm the kind of person who gets a kick from seeing my name in the phonebook. While I was discreetly admiring the pile, and marvelling at how strange life was – by rights I should still be working in an accounts office – I saw a girl pick up a book with my name on it. Casually she glanced at the front, turned it over and read the back. Then – with me holding my breath – she started to drift towards the cash-desk, still with the book in her hand.

Slowly, slowly, she made her way through the shop, while beads of sweat broke out on my forehead. When she finally got to the till and put the book down, this was the real moment of truth. Either she'd brought it over to complain that the bookshop was stocking a load of crap or else she was going to buy it. I could hardly believe it when she began to rummage in her bag for her purse. In a matter of seconds, she'd handed over some money and left with the book. I'm sure she wondered who the weird woman staring at her was, but it made my week.

Adapted from an article first published in *ESB Magazine*,
September 1999.

In the Name of Research – Going Under Cover

When I decided to set my fifth novel in a women's magazine, my friend Morag invited me to do a week's research on the glossy Irish monthly she edited . . .

Day One
I'm ready for my freebies, Mr de Mille.

Up at six trying to Pull Together a Look – have to hold my own with the glam mag folk. Leaving the house, was convinced I cut a fairly impressive dash: until I arrived at the office and clocked the staff. (The prettiness! The skinniness! The lovely shoes!) The scales fell from my (incorrectly made-up) eyes and I saw myself for the lumpen hick I was all along.

But no time to wallow in my rough-hewn crapness – it was straight to work. My first glamorous job was to . . . type in copy! I sat in my best clothes and inputted an article on thrush. Then an article on the new celibacy. All the while I eyed a basket of Charles Worthington products. Would anyone be wanting them? Surely not? Don't they get stuff like that all the time . . . ?

Then Morag interrupted my reverie. 'I need you to do something important.'

I straightened up, my face serious.

And she was right, I thought, as I headed off to the newsagent's. Keeping the workers in cigarettes and chocolate is *very* important.

And so passed my first morning. After lunch (sandwiches from the deli, I went for them), things hotted up when Morag took me to one of Dublin's coolest hotels for a launch party for a groovy new clothes shop.

It quickly became apparent that I Hadn't a Clue. First of all, Morag had to warn me off being excited. Apparently, that's just not *on*. Then I got into trouble for wanting to be on time. Apparently, that's not on either. Then when we walked into the hotel and an Adonis relieved me of my coat, she berated me for that also. You see, you never take off your coat because you want to give the impression that you're just dropping in for a minute.

When we signed the visitors' book, she ran a French-manicured nail along the other signatures and murmured, 'Always check who's here.'

'So we know who to meet?'

'So we know who to avoid,' she corrected sternly.

And then we were in! There was champagne, there were canapés, there were semi-famous Irish people, there was a quite boring speech . . .

Before the applause had even died away, Morag was tugging me out of there. As we left they gave her a little parcel. Some sort of freebie! I turned an eager face to them and – after a slight hesitation – they handed one over to me too. I was thrilled. *Thrilled*.

Morag wouldn't let me open it until we were well clear of the hotel. It turned out to be a T-shirt with the name of the shop and its Irish opening date. Morag was wearily unimpressed. Unlike me.

'But will you wear it?' she asked.

'Well, no,' I admitted. But that was hardly the point, was it? I mean, it had been *free*. I'd got a *freebie*!

Then we had to go for coffee. Morag was going to a charity dinner that evening and needed sustenance before she could face the traffic home to put on her fabulous frock and come back into town.

Sitting in the café, she suddenly sprang to her feet and pelted out into the street. In seconds she was back, with a man in tow. She introduced him as Donald, part of the design duo, Oakes.

'Lend us a dress,' she beseeched Donald, 'so I don't have to go home to get ready.'

'Sure,' he said expansively. 'Call round to the shop and pick one out. But how will you manage for shoes?'

By way of answer, Morag pulled a pair of strappy sandals from her bag. Her emergency pair. I was EXTREMELY impressed.

Day Two

My first task of the day was one of monumental importance: I had to pick the winners for the mountain-bike competition by putting my hand in a sack and emerging with five envelopes. I let my hand hover in the darkness, willing it to pick the right people, the *worthiest* people. Morag watched wryly.

Then it was my great honour to ring the five lucky contestants and break the good news to them. To my disgust, all I got were answering machines — why couldn't they have given their work numbers? Finally, on my fifth phone call, I got a real person and I must say, he did sound very grateful. I may have even detected a catch in his voice. He told me he'd been having a bad run of luck and that he hoped my phone call was a sign that everything was about to change.

After the high emotion of that, I inputted more text (all the while admiring the basket of Charles Worthington products) until it was time to leave for the National Spinach Week lunch. (I'm not making this up.) It was being held in a fancy-dan restaurant I'd always wanted to go to and it was, of course, lovely. My only quibble was that it featured a quite astonishing amount of spinach. A spinach-rich starter, spinach soup, a spinach-centric main course (with a side order of spinach) and — ahaha! — spinach ice-cream for dessert. If only I liked spinach . . .

Speeches followed, then a cookery demo — featuring guess what? — and it was mid-afternoon before we made our escape. After I'd dropped into M&S for a sandwich (I had to, I was starving), Morag whisked me into Brown Thomas for a make-up demo from an expensive cosmetic company. The girl demonstrated how to wear the new season's slap — very interesting, far, *far* more complicated than I'd ever realized — then she parcelled up a desirable selection into a dinky little case and handed it to Morag. I turned my eager face on to the girl — well, it had worked the day before with the T-shirt. But nothing doing, no freebies forthcoming and I felt strangely sullen. I mean, the new shop had given me a T-shirt, what was wrong with this stingy lot?

Day Three

No typing today, oh ho, no! Much more challenging work on the agenda — 'headers'. You know the couple of sentences that are beneath a headline and above the article — that's a header. Easy, you might think. Wrong, wrong, wrong! Very, very hard. Much harder than it seems, you know. I spent a good hour and a half trying to come up with a snappy, grabby intro to a cookery piece. 'If your custards are crap and your stir-frys are shite . . .' No. Start again. 'If your roasts are rotten and your soufflés suck . . .' No, no, NO.

Eventually, Morag swung by and without even breaking stride called out two perfect sentences — lyrical, appropriate, effortless. Call myself a writer!

But no time to beat myself up. I was off *on my own* to the launch of a new range of tights. I made myself be ten minutes late, I held on to my coat, but as soon as they gave me a badge that said 'press' there was no holding back my excitement.

There was champagne, canapés and — I couldn't help but

notice – the same people who'd turned up to the other publicity events. The Liggeratti. Then, to my astonishment, the lights were dimming, and before I knew what was happening we were plunged into a floor show to showcase the new tights. Flashing lights and skirt-free dancing girls, and songs about legs: ZZ Top's 'Legs' and Rod Stewart's 'Hot Legs' and much more besides. As the coloured lights played over my face, I experienced a chink of uncertainty. If I hadn't been so sure that all this was highly glamorous, I might have thought it a bit naff and dreadful.

As I left, I promised a lovely mention in the magazine and the PR girl looked at me like I was insane. Too late, I remembered what Morag had told me. Never, ever promise a PR girl that you'll give them coverage. Even if you're planning to. Apparently it's Just Not On.

I stuck my hand out for my free gift: a sweatshirt advertising the tights. To my shame I wasn't impressed. Three days and already I'd become blasé.

Day Four

Proof-reading. Very, very important. Morag put the fear of God in me by telling me what had happened on one of the other magazines she'd worked on. A recipe for a Christmas cake should have said ½ pound of butter, but went to press as 12 pounds. Apparently, tens of thousands had to be paid out in compensation.

Handily for my book, one of the other girls chipped in with a horror story of her own – a knitting pattern had gone to press with a superfluous zero and mammies the length and breadth of Ireland ended up knitting jumpers whose sleeves were eight feet long.

Then there was a meeting to finalize that month's cover. The graphics person moved text around and changed background colour and I made what I thought were considered, intelligent comments. My money was on the pink background. 'It's fun,' I enthused. 'It's eye-catching. I'd buy it.'

'Hmmmm,' Morag said, then turned to the graphics person. 'Go with blue.'

Right.

Day Five
The final day.

Made last-minute checks before this month's issue could be put to bed. Ensuring that if the contents list promises that page sixty-six has 'Handbags are the new shoes – fact or myth?' it doesn't turn out to be the article on cystitis, that photos of Germaine Greer aren't captioned with 'Robbie Williams, our favourite cheeky chappie', *that* sort of thing.

Then I sat in on a meeting with Morag and deputies while they flatplanned the next edition. This was both easier and more difficult than I'd expected. Some things are givens – like horoscopes and books pages. But other stuff – like interviews and features – is trickier. There has to be the right balance of serious and light. And if a rival mag has covered something or someone recently, it immediately becomes as untouchable as radioactive waste. Very, very difficult. They asked me if I had any suggestions. After pretending to give it some thought, I asked ultra-casually, 'Will you be doing any hair-care pieces . . . ?'

My last duty was that evening — attending a big, televised fashion show. When I realized I was seated three rows from the stage, I tried to look world-weary and unimpressed. I suspect I made a bad job of it. Within seconds of the x-ray-skinny models starting their march down the catwalk, I was plunged into a fierce determination never to eat again. Other than that, I had a great time.

As I got up to leave, I tucked my basket of Charles Worthington products under my arm, but Morag had one final piece of advice for me. She murmured discreetly that I shouldn't say that I thought the models wearing Dries Van Noten looked like they'd been at the dressing-up box. It Just Wasn't On.

Previously unpublished.

Planes, Trains and Ought-to-know-betters

*I*t was six in the morning and perishing cold. I was in Newcastle-upon-Tyne station, waiting for the Transpennine Express to take me to Manchester. As the train inched into the station, the multitude on the platform surged forward and it became clear that I wouldn't be needing my first-class ticket. Because, once again, the train had no first-class compartment. Ah, the joys of book promotion! I'd already spent ten days traipsing up and down the UK, publicizing *Rachel's Holiday*. Even though Penguin had furnished me with first-class tickets for every journey, they were shag-all use to me if the train was like the Dart (Dublin's version of the Underground).

And off to Manchester for Evelyn the publicity girl and me. The train was *exactly* like a Dart. Especially in terms of speed, catering trolleys and, above all, 'comfort' facilities (in other words, there was no loo). We stopped at every single station on the 220-mile stretch of track.

Things got good in York, when an entire department of telesales girls got on, on a works outing to the *Coronation Street* studios in Manchester. A girl who called herself 'Mandeh' sat beside me and told me her life story. I heard of her fiancé

Nigel, whom she relieves of his wages every Friday night, so that if he wants to go out on the sauce he has to ask Mandeh for money. 'Treat 'em mean,' she muttered grimly. 'Keep 'em keen,' I finished for her. She stared at me in surprise. 'Eeh, I never heard that before,' she said. 'How's it go again?'

Next, Mandeh held forth in an extremely loud voice about the injustice of someone called 'Emileh' getting three Saturdays off in a row, while poor Mandeh hadn't had a Saturday off in a month. 'Like as like, luv, it weren't pigging *fair*,' she complained, staring hard at a cringing woman whom I took to be Emileh.

Many hours later, we arrived in Manchester. After I'd sprinted to the Ladies' we were met by a plump, balding man called Ernie who drove us to a town about two hours south of Manchester, where I was doing a book signing. Ernie had driven all the 'greats' in his time, he informed me – Tom Jones, Abba, Engelbert Humperdinck, even President Jimmy Carter. 'Although he wasn't the president at the time,' Ernie admitted. 'But Tom Jones – I saved his life. Crowds of women, hysterical for him, and I got him away to safety. They'd have *killed* him. But what a way to die . . .' Ernie suddenly went all wistful and silent.

The bookshop was in a pedestrian precinct, which concerned Ernie greatly. 'I'm not sure I can get the car around to the back entrance,' he said anxiously. 'Normally I'd be able to get you in via the goods-inwards part, but I'm not sure we can manage it this time.' Baffled, I told him that the front door of the shop would do fine and he blanched. 'But the crowds,' he said, panic-stricken. 'I know! I've a blanket in the boot. We can cover you with that and Evelyn and I will rush you through. I'll radio ahead and let them know you're coming.' His eyes were narrowed in anticipation and it was clear there was a film running in his head where the part of Ernie was being played by Clint Eastwood.

'Marian will be fine,' Evelyn spelt out gently for him. 'People who come to book signings aren't like people who go to Tom Jones concerts.' Reluctantly, sulkily, Ernie gave in, and watched Evelyn and me walk the ten yards to the bookshop, shaking his head, prophesying that no good would come of this. And he was right, although not in the way that he'd anticipated.

Book signings are a tricky business. I've done some where a queue forms an hour before I arrive, and I've done others where no one comes at all. Like this one.

I sat at a mahogany table, almost obscured by unsold copies of *Rachel's Holiday*, and fixed a rictus grin on my face for a very long time. I amused myself by watching the tumbleweed blow up and down the shop. Eventually, after what seemed like several hours, a man approached me. My heart leapt, then plummeted again when it turned out that he just wanted to know where the science-fiction section was. Many millennia later, an elderly woman came up to the table. 'Where are the Diana books?' she demanded. I explained to her that I didn't work there, so I couldn't help her. 'Well, what are you doing sitting here if you don't work here?' She was outraged. Meekly, I tried to explain the concept of book signing to her.

'So you've written this book?' she finally grasped. 'Well, would I like it?' I thought of the scenes of debauched drug-taking and dangerous sex in *Rachel's Holiday*, then I looked at the woman, at her grey, fleece-lined moon boots, her transparent plastic raincoat, her brown string shopping bag. 'Yes,' I said firmly. 'You'd love it!'

Then I asked her what she was called so that I could sign the book for her. 'Oh no, I'll not tell you my name,' she said triumphantly. 'They say Big Brother is watching you. Well, he's not watching *me*.' Then she scooped up the book and left the shop without paying.

Time to go, but no sign of Ernie. Evelyn's phone rang. It was Ernie. He was round the back, had finally managed to get the car there. I gave a last sorrowful look at the entirely empty shop, before being led through labyrinthine corridors and a grey metal fire door into the outside world.

Among the loading bays, bins and cardboard boxes, Ernie stood holding a blanket. He looked like a bull-fighter. 'No!' Evelyn shouted at him, as he made to bag me. 'Ah, boo,' Ernie pouted, putting the blanket aside and kicking at non-existent stones.

Back to Manchester. Radio stations, journalists, more book-shops, each visit delayed by half an hour as Ernie *insisted* on negotiating Mancunian traffic jams to bring me to the back entrance of wherever I was going.

Hours and hours later I finally got to bed. I turned out to be staying at the Granada Hotel, literally across the road from the *Coronation Street* set. (I had a quick look for Mandeh, but no sign.) The road was festooned with enormous, neon decorations bearing the faces of the Corrie cast. From my window it looked like Las Vegas. I fell asleep with the benign face of Curly Watts smiling in on top of me.

And before I knew it, it was time to get up and get the Dart to Nottingham.

First published in *Irish Tatler*, May 1998.

Fear and Loathing in Los Angeles

I'd never flown first class. Then my life took a turn for the unexpectedly glamorous when the Disney Corporation flew me to Los Angeles for three days (*three days!*) to discuss adapting one of my novels into a mooooo-vie. Virgin Atlantic first class was everything I had ever imagined and *more*. The seats were enormous and reclined so much it was just like being in bed.

Across the aisle there was a groovy bloke with dreadlocks and Shaft-type flares. He wore his shades *for the entire flight*. 'Who's that eejit?' I wondered. I later discovered he was Lenny Kravitz. As I snuggled up in my double-bed-sized seat, I experienced a pang for my old friend Paul Whittington who was also LA-bound, but in economy class on Air France. 'There but for the grace of God,' I murmured.

After we took off, the hostess asked me if I wanted to be woken for lunch. I asked her to wake me for everything, and so she did. A back massage, an eighteen-course lunch, a goodie bag of Molton Brown cosmetics, an Aero ice-cream, hot chocolate-chip cookies, fruit kebabs, cashew nuts, *Fear and Loathing* on my personal telly. When we arrived in LA twelve hours later, I didn't want to leave. Even now, if I'm having a bad day, I pretend I'm back there and suddenly things seem copeable-with again.

In arrivals I was met by a chatty Hungarian in a limo. He got through cigarettes at a fierce rate and I subsequently discovered he was the last remaining smoker in LA – smoking is illegal in all bars and restaurants. While I tried to take that in, we passed a crowd of Hare Krishnas doing a lack-lustre chant outside Pan Am.

It was fearsomely hot as we drove along and the grey glare hurt my eyes. The sky looked like it could do with a good scrub with a wire brush. Abruptly I realized what was so odd – there were no human beings on the streets. The place had a strange science-fiction feel to it. And the shops were weird. Gun shops, spy shops selling surveillance equipment, liquor stores and many, many orthodontists. Half an hour later we got to my hotel, which was a bizarre and fabulous Art Deco tower on Sunset Strip (*Sunset Strip!*). As soon as the limo drew to a halt, an astonishingly handsome young man, with perfect hair, an exquisitely cut suit and a strange, orange, plastic-type look about him tap-tapped down the hotel steps and, with a deferential flourish, opened the car door for me. Meanwhile, at the top of the steps, another orange plastic young man had already opened the hotel door and was waiting with an over-obsequious expression. Yet another young man was eagerly wresting my luggage from the boot of the car.

Instantly, I went into tipping frenzy. Whenever I go to the US, I live in such terror of undertipping or not tipping when I should have done that I have a constant knot in my stomach and tip anything that moves. If I was mugged I would probably press a dollar into my attacker's hand. Disney had given me a daily allowance to cover food, cars and, of course, tips. I managed to spend most of it in the walk from the car to the door of the hotel. Dollar bills flurrying everywhere. After I checked in, another young man pressed the button to call the lift and I went into a small spasm about whether I should tip him too. Feck it, I thought, why leave him out?

My ninth-floor room was actually a suite. With its original Art Deco furniture, features and proportions it was beyond amazing. It had sweeping views over the awesome megalopolis of LA. Directly below me the Hockneyesque hotel swimming pool winked and twinkled in turquoise invitation. *I can't believe I'm here*. A little girl from Dublin, who the hell do I think I am?

There was a message to meet the producer and his staff for dinner in Maple Drive, which the guidebook described as one of the best restaurants in Beverly Hills. This made me want to lie down in a darkened room with a cool cloth on my forehead. Instantly, every item of clothing I'd brought – and there were an awful lot of them – seemed inappropriate. I'm not worthy, I thought over and over. I had to go out to buy something.

Disoriented and jet-lagged, I lurched along in the ninety-degree heat, my legs feeling as though they were sinking up to my knees into the pavement. And it was then that I discovered that it really is true that no one, *no one*, walks in

LA. I was a one-woman freak show and the Sunset Strip traffic slowed down to stare incredulously at me. I turned back.

Later, when my cab drew up outside Maple Drive, a crowd of young men surged upon me. For a moment I thought it was my lucky day, then I discovered they were that odd breed of human beings – valet parkers. They fell back when they realized there was nothing for them to park.

In the restaurant the prices were entrail-freezingly high. The waiter, another firm-jawed, orange plastic type told us about the day's specials. 'We have a miso broth which is a low-sodium, lactose-friendly, dairy-free, vegan soup. It has zero, read my lips, *zero* fat content and comes in at fifty calories a serving. We also have a pumpkin risotto, which is a yeast-free, candida-friendly, vegan dish' . . . And so on, *ad infinitum*. He could have won an Oscar for his delivery.

When Julie the scriptwriter, who'd flown in from New York, ordered a steak, there was an appalled intake of breath. Red meat! Meanwhile, the Angelenos ate *nothing*, just fiddled abstemiously with a piece of dressing-free radicchio. There was one bottle of wine between a table of six. It's not that they're mean, you understand – on the contrary. But nobody drinks.

The next day, we went to the producer's beautiful house to 'bounce around some ideas'. He lived in Brentwood, which is a lush, moneyed area, home to people like O. J. Simpson. The houses are all enormous, mostly Spanish-style, with exotic, palm-treed gardens, pools and 'Armed Response' signs. Electronic gates were the order of the day.

After we'd bounced until we could bounce no more, I went to Shutters on the Beach, a spectacular restaurant on the beach in Santa Monica, to bond with the scriptwriter. I was torn because, while it was fabulous there, it was Paul Whittington's birthday and he was celebrating it in a bar which was rumoured to turn a blind eye to smoking.

The following day I was to meet the producer on the Disney lot. When I asked where exactly his office was, I received the reply, 'On the corner of Mickey Avenue and Dopey Drive.' 'HAHAHAHA!' I roared. 'Stop it, you're a hoot. Tell me the real address.'

'That is the real address,' he replied in a small, perplexed voice.

So we did indeed meet on the corner of Mickey Avenue and Dopey Drive and made our pitch to a thirteen-year-old executive. And before I knew it, it was time to get back on the plane. As I snuggled gratefully beneath my Virgin Atlantic duvet, I couldn't take my eyes off one of the other passengers – a middle-aged woman wearing a strange gingham suit and a yeehaw belt slung low on her hips. 'Who's your *one*?' I thought in astonishment.

It was Vivienne Westwood.

First published in *Irish Tatler*, February 1999.

27

If it's Wednesday, it Must be Hamburg

Every now and then I go to furrin parts to promote books. When I was on tour in Germany and Austria, promoting the German edition of Last Chance Saloon, Irish Tatler *asked me to keep a diary. This is it . . .*

Hamburg. Saturday Night

We've collected our baggage and are speeding away in a taxi ten minutes before we're supposed to land. God, I love German efficiency. It's easy to make fun of the Germans (go on, try it if you don't believe me), but I'm very fond of them. Have arrived in Hamburg for a five-day publicity tour and it's going astonishingly well so far. Starting when we turned up at the Lufthansa desk at Heathrow and they actually had us booked on the flight!

At ten-fifteen we arrive at the Hotel Vier Jahreszeiten (apparently the second-best hotel in the world), and are shown into a five-room suite which is bigger and far nicer than our house at home. 'By the living jingo,' exclaims Himself (who has been let come with me), 'but we've landed on our feet this time!'

A knock on the door and a waiter is carrying in a bucket

of Veuve Cliquot. Another knock and a woman is presenting me with an armload of flowers. Another knock and both Himself and myself are invited to select a fancy shower gel – he picks Hermés, I pick Trésor. Just as I think I've died and gone to heaven, there's another knock on my door and it's the arrival of my schedule for the next five days. That wipes the smile off my face, let me tell you. Busy is one way of describing it. Inhuman might be another.

Sunday Morning

Free time to wander around the shops of Hamburg – but they're all closed! I thought Germans had a reputation for being hard workers. Well, I'm here to tell you it's a big cod. All sorts of fabulous shops and not a single one of them open. Scratched pathetically and whimpered at the door of the Prada shop. (Actually, I'm only showing off here. If it had actually been open I'd have been way too intimidated to cross the threshold.)

Sunday Afternoon

Met Yvonne, the publicity girl who'll be travelling with me and minding me for the five days. Luckily, she's a dote. And then, it's showtime! The minute the first interview started I remembered with a sudden sinking heart: a) how much I hate doing interviews, and b) how much harder it is doing them across the language divide. If you say to an Irish journalist, 'I'd love to have children but you can be damn sure I'll be mainlining heroin at the birth,' they don't tend to reply,

'Heroin? But I am vorried vot it will do to your baby.' And when I hurriedly explain to Fritz that I don't actually intend to mainline heroin, it's just that I'm not keen on pain, he looks at me in confusion and says, 'Ah! So it vos a lie?' 'No,' I explain desperately. 'Not a lie. A joke! Joke. Funny. Hahaha.' But my attempt to do a charades-style enactment of a joke falls on barren ground.

I'd also forgotten how much more seriously German journalists treat interviews with authors. For a start, they've all read the book (almost *unheard* of in England or Ireland). And their questions are so much more intense. 'Vot is the secret of heppiness?' several of them asked. While I flapped around trying to come up with an answer, I yearned for a journalist to ask me what colour my pants were.

Sunday Evening
Tonight we had dinner with the woman who translates my books from English to German and I was so happy to be with someone who spoke fluent English that I almost burst into tears.

Monday
Interview after interview after interview after interview. They just kept coming. Before I was finished with one journalist another would be hovering in the doorway looking meaningfully at me. And every single one of them had been to Ireland on their holiers. 'Yes, I know Letterfrack.' 'Yes, I know Doolin.' 'Yes, I know Buncrana.' (I said those sentences a *lot*

during the course of that long, long day.) There was a time when I used to think there could be nothing nicer than talking about yourself all day long. But since I've become a writer and started going on publicity tours I've changed my mind. It actually sends you temporarily bonkers. In the midst of my umpteenth conversation about how the Celtic Tiger has changed Ireland (with specific reference to Letterfrack, Doolin or Buncrana), my head lifted and I heard my voice echoing from far away. My first out-of-body experience of the tour.

When the last interview finished my mouth was cotton-wool dry and I was as dazed and exhausted as if I'd been without sleep for several days. I never wanted to speak to anyone else for as long as I lived, but instead I had to put on my party frock and repair to the Abaton cinema where a famous German actress called Ulrike Kriener and I were doing a reading.

To my great delight, over a hundred people turned up. (I've done readings in Ireland where five people have showed and three of them are homeless men who've come in for a sleep.) Doris from the publishers gave the assembled audience a big long introductory spiel about me, but it was all in German so while they writhed in hilarity, I remained sitting on the stage wearing an uncertain smile. *What was she saying about me that was so funny? Was it my big arse? Or my skirt?*

The reading kicked off. Ulrike read in German and I read in English and the audience laughed, which was great. Afterwards when they were invited to ask questions they all went very coy and silent, but a few of them came up afterwards for a chat. It was the high point of the day. Then went for dinner with Yvonne, Ulrike and Doris. A couple of journalists came too, so I had a few more conversations about Ross's Point and Westport. Finally, collapsed into bed at midnight.

Tuesday. Munich

Came to sometime around ten o'clock when we got to our hotel suite. It was fabulous and peculiar – I was awake enough to register that. Even though the hotel was a big, business-type place with marble lobby and Louis Vuitton shop, our suite was done out like an (enormous) Bavarian woodcutter's cottage. All rough-hewn wood, low ceilings, high little windows and chintz Austrian blinds. A couple of over-the-phone radio interviews followed (mercifully in English – the hell of 'simultaneous translation' was still ahead of me in Berlin), then two hour-long newspaper interviews, and then – a cancellation! An hour to stagger around the Marienplatz gawking at the Munich people, wondering what it was like to be them.

Back for three more intense interviews, then off to Café Mufthalle for the evening's reading. TV München were doing a documentary on me, which meant I had to smile constantly from seven till midnight in case they filmed me looking knackered or distracted.

Once again people turned up, once again they laughed (particularly at the introduction. It *is* my arse), and once again they all looked shyly at their shoes when they were asked if they had any questions.

After the reading we went for dinner (still being followed

by TV München's cameras. Have you any idea what it's like eating a hamburger and chips, aware than your every mouthful is being filmed? Actually, what a great way to lose weight!), and at twelve-thirty finally got to bed.

Wednesday. Vienna

It's official. I've died and gone to hell. I've never been so tired in my life. Slumped against the plane window, we flew over snow-covered forests *en route* to Vienna. Vienna is gorgeous, the hotel suite with its upstairs sitting-room and tented day-bed is delicious, but I'm too tired to care.

A couple of interviews before lunch, then got taken out into the snow-swirly streets by a photographer. 'Febulous, febulous! Sharming, febulous,' he encouraged, as he clicked away and I slowly froze to death. Only when the tips of my fingers had actually fallen off with the cold did he let me back to the hotel. (Said that later to a journalist, who stared closely at my hands, then fixed me with a 'Do you take me for a right eejit?' look.)

At one o'clock we had lunch with the Irish Ambassador to Austria. Oh, the joy of being with an Irish person! Said 'Feck', 'Yoke', 'Divil the bit' and 'Ride me sideways' many, many times, safe in the knowledge that I wouldn't have to attempt to provide a fifteen-minute explanation.

Back to the hotel for more interviews. Then at five-thirty we repaired to Molly Darcy's Irish bar for that evening's reading. We were due to start at six, but I warned Ulrike and Yvonne that if there were Irish people involved we'd be lucky to get going by half-six. 'The man who made time made plenty of it,' I tried nervously, but they just didn't get it. And sure enough, because Molly Darcy's were very decently providing the audience with sandwiches, the reading couldn't start without them. At ten past six word came that 'the sandwiches are being cut'. The Austrians and Germans were beyond incredulous (you'd think that after all their holidays in Kinsale and Castlegregory that they'd know what we're like). By contrast, I was thrilled and for a few minutes I savoured the fantasy that I was at home. At twenty past, the first of the sandwiches made their appearance and by half six (just like I'd foretold) we were underway. No official dinner that evening – hurray! Tried to walk around Vienna to see the sights by night, but were driven back by snow. In bed and asleep by ten o'clock.

Thursday. Berlin

Despite my extreme shaggeredness, couldn't help a frisson of excitement as we circled over the (alarmingly large) suburbs of Berlin.

In the taxi on the way to the hotel we passed a bombed-out old church. 'What's that?' I asked.

'A monument to the futility of war,' Yvonne replied.

Two press interviews, then off to DeutschRadio for a live interview with their version of Terry Wogan. We passed a huge abstract sculpture. 'What's that?' I asked.

'A monument to the sorrow of war,' Yvonne replied.

The interview was a pure disaster. The idea was that the

German Terry Wogan would ask the questions in German, they'd be translated into English and spoken into headphones I was wearing, then I'd reply in English and the translator would translate back into German. But due to a technical hitch I could barely hear the English translation, so I couldn't answer the questions. And when I attempted to anyway, I could hear the translator speaking in German in my headphones, which was like having a peculiar echo on the line. God, it put years on me. I thought it would never end!

Going back to the hotel, we passed a crowd of people gathered around something on the ground. 'What are they doing?' I asked.

'They're looking into the empty, underground library,' Yvonne said. 'A monument to the sadness of war.'

Two more interviews, then out for that night's reading. On the way we passed a big, silver building. Yvonne told me it was the Jewish museum. 'A monument to the abhorrence of war.'

The reading went great, the best yet. Then out for dinner. On the way home we passed a crisp packet lying on the pavement. 'What's that?' I asked.

'A monument to the grief of war,' Yvonne replied. 'Oh no,' she recovered herself. 'It's a crisp packet.'

Then home to bed. I'm never speaking to anyone ever again.

First published in *Irish Tatler*, May 2000.

Given the Boot

*T*he minute I got off the plane and set foot on English soil, the heel fell off my boot. With a bit of an undignified skid the majority of the boot decided to head for Arrivals, Terminal One, but the heel decided it was happier staying where it was, thanks.

Suddenly I was listing to one side, like a wrecked ship. So as nimbly as I could (not very), I moved out of the way of all the narky people who'd come crashing into the back of me after my hasty, sliding halt. 'Sorry,' I mumbled, as they marched past, glaring and glowering, hefting their bags of duty-free. I took off my boot to inspect the damage. Critical. The heel was hanging on to the mainland by just a couple of nails. So I limped along to the luggage retrieval and gave the whole sorry mess a good hammer on the carousel. Mercifully the heel went back on, but then I looked inside and saw a tangle of nails erupting up into the boot, like a hernia.

Naïvely, I expect objects to survive until I've had enough of them. I expect them to serve me, to do my every bidding until I choose to cast them aside like a dry husk. Not to mention that I feel the loss of a piece of footwear as I would a close relative. That'll learn me to anthropomorphize things. 'Lookit.' I waved the boot at Himself. 'They're shagged and they're only new!'

'Hardly new,' he said mildly (because that's the kind of man he is).

'They *are* new,' I insisted. 'No more than a year, anyway.'

'More like a year and a half,' he said, offering me his arm as I upped-and-downed along, my foot cold from the floor, my face warm from the embarrassment, my ears burning from the other passengers' sniggers.

'And how am I going to get to the hotel with only one boot?' I demanded.

'Lep up on the trolley there,' he offered. 'I'll push you to the Tube.'

The loss of the boot wasn't a major catastrophe in the overall scheme of things. Except that the following day I was going to a literary lunch, then I was leaving London for Australia and New Zealand in an attempt to convince the good burghers of the Antipodes to buy one of my books. (I'm really sorry if I sound like a big show-off saying that, but they worked me into the ground, I swear, and it took me the best part of six months to get over the jet lag.) It would be cold in New Zealand. The boots were vital.

Unusually for me, I had no other boots about my person. I always bring too much stuff. Even when I go out to buy a pint of milk I overpack. But on this trip, for some insane reason I'd decided to downsize, travel light, *rationalize*, as it were. And look at where it had got me.

'Can't you get a pair in New Zealand?' Himself enquired. But I'd seen a copy of my New Zealand schedule and I had five and a half minutes to myself on the third day and that seemed to be the extent of my time off. No time for buying boots.

'Can't you buy a pair in Australia *before* you get to New Zealand?' he suggested.

'I wouldn't say they sell boots in Australia,' I said doubtfully, thinking of *Home and Away* and *Picnic at Hanging Rock*. I was sure I'd never seen any boots in them. 'Flip-flops, maybe, but I can't imagine them having four-inch-heeled boots.'

Himself mournfully agreed.

But when I opened my case in the hotel, he gestured excitedly at my snakeskin sandals, turquoise suede wedges and silver-speckled jellies. 'But you've *loads* of shoes,' he bellowed joyfully. I shook my head sadly. Men just don't get it, do they? They're definitely missing the shoe chromosome.

Just as we thought all was lost, I narrowed my eyes thoughtfully, stared into the middle distance and breathed, 'I've an idea. It's a long shot but it just might work.'

Operation Early Start involved me getting up at the crack of dawn. Before the shops even opened I was in Oxford Street, hoping to buy a new pair of boots and still get to the literary lunch.

I made straight for my favourite shoe shop and hung around outside waiting for it to open, as a methadone addict would outside a chemist's. To my relief there was already an employee in the locked shop. With anguished face and frantic hand gestures I conveyed to the girl within that time was short and the situation was desperate. With stony face and short, sharp gestures with her first and middle fingers she conveyed to me that she didn't start work until nine-thirty and didn't give a damn how desperate my situation was. Coldly, she turned back to her styrofoam cup of coffee and her apricot danish. 'May it choke you,' I muttered, for a moment thinking I was my mother.

At nine-thirty-one I was in, surveying the wares with a gimlet eye. I found I was looking for a pair as close as possible to my banjaxed ones – despite the way they'd let me down. I am clearly a creature of habit.

But nothing doing. When you've ridiculously small feet like mine, it's well nigh impossible to get a pair of shoes to fit. (As a result I am queen of the insole.) From what I can gather, they get one pair of size thirty-six shoes in London every season. Shop after shop tried to fob me off with boots two sizes too big for me and it was gone twelve before I struck gold and was able to say those magic words, 'Don't pack them, I'll ride them home!'

Within seconds I was in a taxi, heading for the literary lunch. I hadn't been published for long in Britain, it was the first event of this kind I'd been invited to and I was nervous and excited. Good job I had well-dressed feet for it! I stretched my legs out in front of me, all the better to admire the new boots. I turned them to the left and smiled fondly at them. I turned them to the right . . . and the smile faded. Was there some kind of brownish sheen on one of my lovely new black boots? I gave my foot another twist to see it in a different light. With cold horror it dawned on me. How could I have missed it? *They were two different colours*. One a nice, desirable black, the other a nasty, interloper brown.

As soon as I was aware of it, I couldn't imagine how I'd ever missed it. The brown boot glowed with a malign, brown evilness. The black one shimmered with a kind of apologetic, gentle blackness. It was too late to return to the shop, I had to go to the lunch with one black boot and one brown boot. I was *doomed*.

And I was. The pre-lunch drinks reception was a nightmare. Sporting my name badge, sweating neediness, wearing a desperate please-speak-to-me smile, I'd never been more ignored in my entire life. All because of the brown boot. Mind you, I was ignored by the very best! Nick Hornby shook my hand then quickly turned away. Roddy Doyle stared at me then also turned away – not that I blamed him! The empty space around me grew and grew: I seemed to recede from the room. Everyone else was knee-deep in conversation, laughing their heads off, while alone and on the margins, I fancied that my brown boot was neon and ten times its normal size. It was the longest hour I ever endured.

At least when we sat down for lunch I was able to hide my shame beneath the table. And redemption flickered moment-arily as I thought of wearing the new black one with the old unbroken one. But no. Of course not. That would have been too much to hope for, wouldn't it? The brown boot and the broken boot were both left-foot ones.

So I had no choice. I went to New Zealand with one black boot and one brown one.

First published in *Irish Tatler*, October 1997.

MIND, BODY, SPIRIT . . .
AND SHOES

Imeldas, and How to Spot Them

I remember the first time I fell in love. I was fifteen years old and in a department store. Suddenly the breath was knocked from my body, as my eyes fixed on the object of my desire — a pair of four-inch, black-patent platform wedges with an ankle strap.

I wanted them desperately. I felt they'd change me into someone sophisticated and beautiful and make me completely irresistible to Eddie Jackson. But by the time I'd saved up my babysitting money, the shoes were long gone and Eddie Jackson was sporting several hickies that had Karen Baker's teeth marks on them.

Then, to my surprise, I became obsessed by a pair of navy clogs and I learnt a valuable lesson. Men will come and men will go, but there will always be shoes.

In the same way that men are either leg-men, breast-men or I'll-take-what-I'm given men, women are divided into shoe women, bath-products women or nice-underwear women. I'm definitely a shoe woman. Or an Imelda, as we like to call ourselves.

I used to think I was the only one. I lined the floor of my wardrobe with five-inch-heeled gold stilettos, eau-de-nil embroidered leather sandals and flowery Dr Martens and thought I was the only person who had ever slept with their new pair of green nubuck clogs.

Until a new girl started at work, wearing ox-blood pumps with back-to-front heels. 'I love shoes,' she admitted. 'All my friends call me Imelda. After Imelda Marcos.'

I was really upset. I had thought *I* was Imelda. But it transpired that there are lots of us out there and it's better to befriend each other. We're like collectors of rare artefacts. Only an Imelda would murmur, 'I've got a pair of rather special cone-heeled ankle boots that I think you might find interesting.' And only another Imelda wouldn't think she was a total nutter.

If they can't get shoes in the right size, Imeldas will still buy them, if they're sufficiently fabulous. Because there are remedies. Too big? Hey, that's why God invented insoles! Too small? What's a small piece of excruciating agony when your feet are well dressed?

Imeldas pamper their footwear as if they were loyal pets, buying them little titbits, like colour-protect and rain-guard and all the rest of the crap they try to flog you every time you buy shoes. I've got *tons* of those plastic things you stick in shoes to help them keep their shape. And I've spent at least three years of my life holding suede boots over boiling kettles, in a labour of love.

Although recently I met an Imelda who keeps her shoes in their original boxes, and I don't know about you, but I think that's going too far.

Unlike other garments, shoes don't suddenly become too tight one week out of every four. Shoes will still fit you snugly even if you haven't got to the gym for over three weeks and you've been having curries and pizzas every night. You see, shoes deserve your loyalty because they return it.

How to know if you're an Imelda:

~ If you've bought shoes and never worn them because you *didn't want to damage them*.
~ If you structure your day around the shoes you want to wear, staying in when you want to go out, just so you can wear your duck-egg-blue grosgrain slippers.
~ If you've spent more on a pair of shoes than you would on a holiday.
~ If you own around ten almost identical black pairs.
~ If you've ever sustained injury from falling off a high pair *and didn't mind*.
~ If you would rather lie and say you have athlete's foot than loan your shoes to your flatmate.
~ If you've ever slept in a pair – and not because you were so drunk that you couldn't take them off.

Previously unpublished.

Does My Base Chakra Look Big in This?

Rumours had reached us that there was some sort of strange dancing you could do to reactivate your sex life. Image *magazine sent me to investigate . . .*

I might have looked like I was just prancing around a room with ten others, but what I was actually doing was 'Activating Kundalini energy flow in my body, creating a safe, sacred space for healing sexuality.' So now for you.

Tuesday night, Temple Bar, SynergyDance – I had no idea what to expect. Speaking to the teacher, Danielle, beforehand, she had talked of Tantric energy and using dance to release sexuality and bring heightened awareness to mind, body and spirit.

Because of the activating sexuality bit I'd brought Himself, a man who has no time whatsoever for anything even vaguely New Age. He *pleaded* to be absolved from going, but all I could say was, 'You either come with me, or you accept that I may not be responsible for my actions on the bus home.' He came with me.

Riddled with preconception as I am, I had expected the class to be full of outré characters. *Au contraire*, dear reader. It was an object lesson in humility. They weren't part of the crochet-your-own-yoghurt crew, they were perfectly normal-looking women (and one man). Not only that, but they were all slim and attractive – something must be doing them good. To try to find out more about the class, I buttonholed one pupil, a woman with the down-to-earth friendliness of an off-duty nurse. 'It's great fun,' she told me, 'especially the dancing in the second part. You can let go and make a right fool of yourself.'

Then Danielle arrived – and my God, what a babe. She was slender and beautiful and completely relaxed with her body. (Although if my stomach was that flat and my legs that toned, I'd be completely relaxed with my body too, I thought enviously.)

The first hour of the two-hour class involved lying on mats on the floor for a yoga-type visualization. It was actually wonderful. Danielle talked us through a relaxation process starting from our heads and working right down our bodies. The language was lyrical and mystical – much talk of energy, third eyes and golden light radiating from our hearts. When she exhorted us to feel the heat in our base chakra, Himself leant over to me and hissed, 'Where's my base chakra?'

'Your bum,' I whispered back.

It was blissful and not even the tinkle and clatter of the restaurant kitchen over the road could impinge. 'Pass us up dem plates dere, Keith,' a disembodied voice ordered, and I simply snuggled deeper into the golden light.

But then things took a turn for the uninhibited. To release anger and frustration, suddenly we were pounding the floor and ululating like uninhibited Algerians. Well, everyone else was. I wasn't bad at the floor-pounding, but let myself down badly at the ululating. Next we were shoving out a leg like we were kicking a door down in *Starsky and Hutch*. 'Out!' we shouted at the tops of our voices. 'Out! Out!' The regulars were doing it without a trace of self-consciousness. I got as far as mouthing the word but my uptightness wouldn't let me actually articulate it.

I was aware too of the silence emanating from Himself beside me. I couldn't, just *couldn't* look at him, then by accident my eye snagged his and we exchanged a flash of mortification so searing it almost lit up the room.

And then came the Dancing.

This was the bit I'd been dreading. I am Irish, therefore I am inhibited. I don't even like the bit at Mass where we have to exchange the sign of peace with the person beside us, so the thought of 'expressing' myself through free-form movement made me break out in a sweat. What if someone saw me? We began by being orang-utans, moved on to picking imaginary berries, then discarding them, and I have to admit to enduring one of the worst twenty minutes of my life. Woodenly, miserably, I shoved my lumpish, unrhythmic body around the room. On every rotation we passed the clock and I silently begged it to hurry up.

Next we moved on to dancing like the elements, beginning with fire.

'Sparkle like a flame,' Danielle called, waving her arms in a manner that could only be described as flame-like.

I wondered if this was what was going to end my marriage,

but to my great surprise, when I snuck a look at Himself, he was making like a flame like there was no tomorrow. All the others were giving it loads as well.

'Stay grounded,' Danielle said anxiously, and her concern wasn't misplaced because seconds later one of the flames (my husband) went careening into the stereo. He didn't even miss a beat and next minute he was dipping and flowing like a river. (We'd moved on to water.)

Mid-prance we passed each other. He twinkled wickedly at me and grinned, 'Do you feel like a shag?'

'No,' I replied, 'I feel like an eejit.'

However, after a while I kind of got into it. I was never really in danger of going flying into the stereo (not like some I could mention), but that terrible, crippling self-consciousness lifted. I honestly think that if I went regularly or if I did one of the day-long workshops, I'd manage to give my mortification the slip once and for all. And I got a glimpse of the joy the others were experiencing. By now Himself was shaking his hips like a dervish, while I watched in open admiration. In truth, I hadn't known he had it in him.

By the time the class ended, I felt that even if alternative spirituality isn't your bag (man), you can really enjoy yourself if you leave your cynicism at the door. And your ego too, if you can manage it (I obviously couldn't). In fairness though, I can't say it's made any noticeable impact on my sex life. But *somebody* had a good time, because as we got into the car to go home, Himself remarked idly, 'Maybe we should go again.'

*

The following day, I had an appointment at the Harvest Moon Centre with Doctor Yvonne Murphy, who works in tandem with Danielle. She's a fully qualified chiropractor of the conventional medicine kind, but with a difference. She doesn't just fix your gammy back, she 'realigns' your spirit as well. Most of us are 'out of balance' — our male/female sides are skewed or our right brain/left brain balance is off, and once we're back in balance, it'll 'heal sexuality and bring heightened awareness and awake mind, body and spirit'.

The Harvest Moon Centre — like the place the night before — was full of surprisingly normal-looking people: a blonde woman in a black trouser-suit with an umbrella was emerging from having her chakras realigned, a man with the short, tight curls and meaty build of a rugby player was off to the flotation tank for a session. He jerked his thumb towards the tank and casually asked the receptionist, 'I'll just hop in, will I?'

Yvonne took me into a therapy room and within seconds she had discovered the banjaxed bit of my neck. The top of my spine points slightly to the right and I had always thought it was that way because I'd got mild whiplash while on a rollercoaster in Alton Towers. But Yvonne's assessment of it was that my right-brain was working overtime and my left-brain was basically sitting around, slumped in front of the telly, watching Oprah.

She says that our back problems are a map to our emotional and spiritual states. Men mostly come to her with lower-back problems, which means their base chakra — which correlates to survival issues like careers and finances — is giving them gyp.

Her language, like Danielle's, is mystical — the chakra hit-rate per sentence is high. If you were in any way sceptical you might be moved to be scornful and Yvonne is wryly aware that this is the case. Not that she seems to care — if you could bottle her serenity you'd really be on to something. Besides, as she numbers hard-nosed business people among her clientele, she can afford to ignore the sceptics. Accountants and lawyers come to her to get their analytical left-brain to stop bullying the artistic right-brain. Even more intriguingly, greyhound and racehorse owners employ her to work on their animals. In fact, she treats more racehorses than she does human beings! And somehow I can't imagine the horsey set standing for any nonsense if they weren't getting results.

Up on the couch I clambered. At the best of times I'm a massage junkie — call it hands-on healing (Yvonne does) or call it massage, but I love it. With her focus on my neck, skull, face and spine, she twiddled and rubbed me, and it was blissful.

After about twenty minutes of pressure, she told me that my right-brain and left-brain were more in alignment. Honesty compels me to admit that I didn't feel anything that I might describe as a shift, but I didn't care. I felt so good I was floating, and my only regret was that I hadn't been more out of alignment to begin with, because the treatment would have gone on for longer.

When I got home, Himself was waiting for me with eager anticipation.

'Well?' he asked hopefully. 'Is it all systems go?'

I'd ordered him to be on stand-by in case my realignment unleashed a torrent of sexual energy. But your reporter made her excuses and left – I was simply too relaxed. And he balefully muttered something about women always preferring massage to sex.

Later that evening, as we prepared to go out, he limped towards me. 'I think I threw my hip out last night when I was being a gust of air,' he winced.

I had no time for sympathy. 'Tell me,' I said, 'and be honest. Does my base chakra look big in this?'

First published in *Image* magazine, October 1999.

Botox and Other Miracles

Image magazine were doing a special issue focusing on plastic surgery. As I'd just come back from Los Angeles, where I'd been researching my sixth novel, I was the very woman for the job.

I was in Beverly Hills and the woman emerging from the offices of Dr Milton Applebaum had been in a terrible accident, right? Her entire head was swaddled in bandages. Perhaps she was a burns victim. She was being led by a swishy-haired princess who was murmuring tenderly, 'OK, Mom, there's a step coming. Five more steps, then we're there. OK, here's the car. I'm, like, opening the door.' In Mom got, holding her head very gingerly on her neck.

I couldn't help staring. It was such a horrible sight. But the woman wasn't a burns victim, according to my friend Varina.

'Plastic surgery,' she muttered. 'She's had her whole head lifted. You see this a *lot* in Beverly Hills.'

When I opined that it looked painful and disgusting, Varina advised me to get over myself. The woman would spend a couple of days in bed, then have a launch party for her new face.

As we watched mother and daughter drive away, Varina

nodded at the daughter. 'And see her nose? That won't survive in its current configuration for much longer. At Beverly Hills High they get given nose jobs for their sixteenth birthdays.'

Well, I was in Los Angeles, what did I expect? Reconstructive surgery is considered a wonderful thing and a chance to get one over on Mother Nature. Although some people are doomed to disappointment – an earnest young actress confided to me that she'd got her nose done, 'so my kid will be born with a great nose'. Oh dear.

Plastic surgery is on the increase in Ireland, but it still seems to be approached furtively. In Los Angeles they're much more relaxed about it. During my five weeks there, I came across the occasional person going about their business as normal – the only unusual thing was that they had a huge scaffold-type bandage on their nose. At first it made me look – *That person's just had a nose job!* – but by the end of my trip, it was no more remarkable than someone putting a stripe of zinc sun-lotion on their nose.

'And watch out for people wearing sunglasses indoors,' Varina said. 'They've just had their eyes done.' And sure enough, I saw a fair few of them too.

The latest thing seems to be that you have your plastic surgery with your girlfriend. A bonding session that's an alternative to a night out with a few apple martinis, perhaps? In response to this, some surgeons have started offering job-lot price reductions. In fact, the phenomenon has become so popular that there's been a rash of articles in various LA publications about how to deal with jealousy if your friend heals quicker, gets off with the surgeon or just looks better than you when the bandages come off. Everywhere there are ads for tummy tucks, eyelid surgery, lip augmentation, Botox injections, liposuction, collagen replacement therapy, microdermabrasion, chin surgery, forehead lifts and – oh, but of course – breast augmentation.

Forty-six per cent of all breast augmentation in the *entire world* is done in Los Angeles. Of course, everyone knows that LA is the place to spot lots of enlarged breasts, maybe this sounds like old news. But when you actually see them with your own two eyes . . .

A few drinks at The Standard – starlet central – was like being at a freak show. The women were parodies of themselves. It wasn't so much their hand-span waists and childlike hips, it was the enormous, humungous, gravity-defying breasts. They were so obvious and so very, very BIG. And I realized why. If every girl in town has implants, how are you going to distinguish yourself? By going bigger. And statistics support my theory. The size of implants has increased; originally people went up one or two cup sizes, now it's more like three.

Himself is very politically correct and would never comment on a woman's appearance (not unless he wants an elbow in the chops from me), but even he was moved to mutter, 'How come she's upright? How come she's not flat on her face from the weight of those things?'

And as well as being Barbie-proportioned and ever youthful, the other thing Angelenos seem to want is to be entirely bald. Apart from the hairs on their heads, everything must go!

Laser treatment is the thing, claiming to be both permanent and painless. Varina has had it done, and she insists that it's neither. And of course, bikini waxes ranging from 'very little' to 'entirely bare' are hot news. The Brazilian wax – currently big in Ireland – seems to have been overtaken in LA by the Playboy wax, which is even more extreme.

And speaking of extreme . . . *Bleaching* is very now. But I'm not talking about hair. I'm not even talking about teeth. I'm talking about a certain part of one's anatomy that very few people get to see. Delicacy doesn't permit me actually to mention it, but I will say that if you were an exotic dancer who did a lot of bending over, you might get great mileage out of this treatment.

When I was first told about it, I was certain that it was a 'make fun of the credulous Irish girl' joke. But then I saw an actress on a chatshow who'd not only had it done but was willing to speak freely about it, and I had to admit it was for real. I still don't get it though. I'm not entirely averse to the idea of some treatments – a Botox injection doesn't sound so disgusting – but *that* one, it's just too much!

As well as surgery and treatments, the Angelenos' love–hate relationship with food continues apace. (For a group of people who don't eat much, they invest an awful lot of thought in it.) The diet currently big with (so I'm told) Brad Pitt, Jennifer Aniston and other golden Hollywood lovelies is the Zone diet. There have been liquid diets, protein diets, combination diets, fruit diets, and this has to be the most bizarre yet. It features the revolutionary combination of 40 per cent carbohydrates, 30 per cent protein and 30 per cent fat – what I learned in Home Economics was a *balanced diet*. But where's the faddiness? Where's the silliness? How very disappointing that the whole thing has gone full circle.

And if starvation and surgery haven't given you the body you desire, well, then there's always exercise. I joined a gym while I was there and the timetable showed spinning classes at five-thirty. 'Is that five-thirty p.m.?' I asked, fearing the worst. 'No, five-thirty a.m.,' came the reply. 'And if you're coming in the morning, try to get here before seven.' When I enquired why (not that there was a chance it would happen), I was told, 'Because the car-park is full after seven.'

Spinning is still very big there, but the spinning classes here are as nothing compared to the spinning classes there. They are possibly the most savage, inhumane thing that could ever happen to a person. They're high-speed, intense, sustained work. But what was interesting was how regulars coped. A lot of them seemed to go into a type of trance; they pedalled with their eyes closed, seemingly impervious to the tortures being inflicted on their bodies. It put me in mind of the religious ecstasies that people go into when they're being nailed to a cross in a re-creation of the crucifixion, where they really do *feel no pain*. But as well as burning off two thousand calories before breakfast, what is very popular is 'realignment'. Pilates, yoga, and a new combination of the two called yogilates are used to change your posture so that you look taller, thinner and 'more centred'. Varina has a personal 'realigner' who uses a gyrotonic machine and anti-gravity boots (basically, you hang upside-down like a bat) to stretch and straighten her. And what is absolutely huge in LA – and I predict will take off in Ireland soon – is power yoga. It's yoga Jim, but not as we know it. For a start, you don't want to begin screaming with boredom five minutes into it. (Or is it only me who has this problem?) It's done in sauna-hot conditions, so that you detox as you work, and it's *extremely* hard. You don't lose weight with it but it lengthens your muscles, so you look leaner and tauter. They swear by it.

A couple of quickies before I finish – eyebrow shaping. They're all at it, because if it's done right it's 'as good as a face-lift'. (But, obviously, without the *Return of the Mummy* bandages.) If you don't have regular appointments with Anastasia of Beverly Hills, eyebrow shaper to the stars, you might as well get on the bus and go back to Wisconsin.

And finally, nails. I found some of the ways they interfered with their bodies a bit too much, but I really approve of their attitude to nails. Everywhere there are nail salons where you can walk in without an appointment and – here's the good bit – have your hands and feet done *simultaneously*. You read a magazine while one person beautifies your feet and another does your hands. Half an hour later you leave, twenty dollars lighter, with twenty perfect nails. Now the sooner *that* comes to Ireland, the better.

First published in *Image* magazine, October 2000.

Hope Springs Eternal

Occasionally real life leaks into my novels. Anyone who has read Last Chance Saloon *might recognize what happens here . . .*

As the warm three days that constitute the Irish summer will be upon us any minute now, naturally my thoughts turn to shifting the lard from my thighs, bum and the rest of the usual suspects. As always, I've left it far too late for the dieting and exercise lark, so I'm on the lookout for a magic solution. Although I've learnt the hard way that there are no quick fixes. The old Chinese proverb springs to mind – No pain, no gain.

I'm forever placing my faith in a snake-oil salesman of a beautician and I'm forever being disappointed. Let me tell you about the time I went for a body-wrap. A few days before I got married, I decided to 'perspire away those unwanted inches'. I had no choice, because I had made the great mistake of arranging my wedding day for 29th December. Which meant, of course, that the previous six months' hard-won weight-loss was annihilated in a matter of minutes on Christmas Eve, when I interfaced with a wheelie-bin-sized tin of Roses. I should have simply cut out the middle-man and sellotaped those chocolates directly on to my hips, because that's where they went anyway. Unfortunately, my wedding dress wasn't a huge meringue that hid any last-minute expansion in my girth. It was as unforgiving as it was slender and desperate measures were called for. I couldn't locate a back-street liposuctionist at such short notice, so when someone suggested that I had a mud-wrap, I almost wept with gratitude.

I knew about mud-wraps, and I liked what I'd heard. The idea of a full-body immersion in warm, creamy chocolate-type stuff, so that I was like a human Mars Bar, sounded like heaven. And as for the idea of just lying there, losing weight, letting the mud do all the work!

It got better – the beauty salon said they guaranteed a minimum loss of eight inches. *Eight inches!*

Walking on air, thinking of losing four inches from my arse and two from each of my thighs, I went along to the salon two days before the nuptials. Where I met a beautician called Tanya who was clearly displeased at having to come to work two days after Christmas. My mood dipped instantly, as I felt cruel and guilty.

It dipped even further when she ushered me into a freezing little room – clearly they hadn't had the heat on in days – and ordered me to strip off. 'But we've only just met!' I tried to cover my embarrassment with humour, but Tanya ignored me and pulled hard on both ends of her measuring tape, as if she was getting ready to thrash me.

She measured me about fifty different times – each arm

alone was done in four different locations: wrist, forearm, lower upper arm, upper upper arm. Quickly I did my sums, and I didn't have to be Carol Vorderman to figure out that if I lost a fifth of an inch from each measuring place, the promised eight inches wouldn't be too hard to come by, but would make no difference *at all* to my silhouette. The prospect of me walking down the aisle in my lovely white dress seemed less and less likely.

Next, Tanya was using her hand to scoop water out of a bucket and splash me with it. I recoiled in shock – the water was stone cold! 'Oh, didn't I say? The hot water's broken,' Tanya said brusquely, eyeing my goose pimples. When I was finally drenched, she produced a spatula and used it to smear me randomly with a warm, foul-smelling mix.

'That's the mud?' I asked uncertainly.

''Course! What did you think it was?'

So much for the full-body immersion and being a human Mars Bar.

Then she wrapped my legs, arms and midriff in ragged, old, salmon-pink bandages – the sort my mother used to practise her First Aid routines with – and secured each bandage with the kind of pins that normally live on kilts. I felt like such a gobshite.

'Now,' she declared, 'we'll put you into the special rubber suit, which heats up the mud, stimulating your metabolism and increasing weight loss.' Suddenly I was happy again – this sounded reassuringly scientific. A lot more so than kilt pins and spatulas. But the special rubber suit wasn't a special rubber suit at all. All it was was a cheap, nasty shell-suit that a twelve-year-old boy might wear to Funderland. Then she announced that it took about an hour to 'stimulate the toxins'. Basically, what she meant was that her 'full leg and bikini' had arrived, so off she went, abandoning me in the freezing room. To pass the time, I listened to the wince-making rips of the other customer having her legs waxed and wondered which of us felt worse.

Me, probably. Because after a while the bandages cooled and felt damp and clammy under the nylon pants. I was transported back through time to when I was five years old and had wet my knickers.

Some time later, Tanya returned, unpeeled the bandages and measured me again, this time pulling the tape measure so tight she was in danger of arresting my circulation. She seemed in much better form – maybe she'd worked off some of her anger on the leg wax – and offered exclamations of delight at how much I'd shrunk. 'Would you look at that! You're disappearing on us. You're barely there!'

It was bad enough being swizzed. But to be patronized into the bargain . . .

The upshot of it was that she told me I'd lost ten inches. On account of not living in a parallel universe, I couldn't see *any* improvement.

And there was one final twist of the knife: I had expected to have a shower before I got dressed and went home. I had visualized sluicing away my toxins and nasty, evil fat cells in the cleansing, purifying water. But Tanya insisted that I wasn't to wash the muck off yet, because it would continue to detoxify me for a day or so. Any fool could tell that she was only saying that because the hot water was broken, but after paying thirty-five quid for the experience, I thought I might as well get what I could out of it. So I put my clothes on over the mud, gave her a hefty tip and left, bitterly disappointed.

That evening, my family-in-law-to-be came to my parents' house to get jarred and bond with each other before the wedding. And I yielded dried mud with every movement. A trail of brown dust followed me, as if I was rotting. Whenever anyone brushed against me, dried mud billowed forth, as though I'd just been exhumed. Each time I passed my future father-in-law a drink, a cloud of dust rose from me, obscuring my view of him. If someone sat beside me, their nose wrinkled in surprise at the stench surrounding me, and they quickly got up and moved elsewhere.

Anyway, the good news is that through no fault of my own I still managed to fit into my wedding dress. The bad news is I saw a feature about mud-wraps on telly recently. And although I know the truth, I was *still* sucked in. Seduced by the thought of a quick fix. Hope springs eternal . . .

Previously unpublished.

What Colour is Your Aura?

Like every other magazine at the time, Irish Tatler *had a special so-what-did-you-think-of-the-nineties? edition. This was my contribution.*

*E*arlier this year, I was at a friend's house and sitting beside me was a woman I'd never met before. She was great fun and had nice shoes and I thought she was lovely. Next thing she started rummaging around in her handbag, located a red bindi (small round yoke that women in India wear on the forehead to signify what caste they belong to, I think) and stuck it between her eyes. 'That's better,' she sighed. 'Now it's closed.' She turned to me and explained, 'My third eye has been giving me terrible gyp. I've been getting all sorts of unwanted insights and psychic flashes.'

This is the kind of behaviour that once could have got you arrested. Or at the very least, ferried off in the bouncy ambulance to a high-security laughing house. But it's a testament to how codology-friendly the nineties are that I just nodded and smiled (and moved my chair away a little, but still).

There was a time in Ireland when, if you were looking for

some kind of a spiritual fix, you'd have your tarot cards read. Or else you'd make a ouija board or get your mammy to do a novena, and that really was all that was available to you. You had superstitions, of course – like you wouldn't stir your tea with a knife, or if you spilt salt, you'd throw some more over your left shoulder, but superstitions are more *preventative* than *proactive*, if you follow me.

But look at how things have changed. Once upon a time, if you said you heard voices in your head, everyone thought you were schizophrenic. But now you're as likely to be talking about your 'spirit guides' as needing very strong medication.

Codology abounds on the island of Saints and Scholars! Irish interiors magazines cover the Feng Shui issue with nary a hint of irony. The radio programme *Live-line*, which usually deals with practical issues like bin collection, recently gave airspace to a woman who claims she is followed constantly by a veritable posse of guardian angels visible only to (you'll never guess!) herself. The annual Mind, Body and Spirit fair in Dublin offers, among other things, rebirthing, colour therapy, dream interpretation and some bollocks with pyramids (and lovely frozen yoghurt, but I digress). Not too many years ago, the likes of this fair would probably have been picketed by a crowd of foam-flecked 'Christians', who for a long time claimed a monopoly on all things spiritual in Ireland. But now that spirituality has been deregulated, the joint was jumping with people enthusiastically embracing a plethora of psychic balm. Indeed, I'm not ashamed to admit (well, only a little) that I had my aura photographed. (A lot of purple and white – apparently that means I'm artistic, which just shows how wrong they can be.)

Most of this stuff seems to kick off in Southern California. Los Angeles, in particular, seems to be the original life-source of nearly all things codologistic, with a self-renewing well bubbling constantly to the surface. I can't shake an image of a think-tank of Los Angelenos sitting around appropriating Eastern, Native American and Amazonian carry-on and reshaping and marketing them into the Next Big Thing. It's no coincidence that Los Angeles is also the most mammon-obsessed, materialistic place on earth. Your car is the most important thing about you. And your teeth. Oh yeah, and your aura . . .

When I was in Los Angeles, one of the new notions doing the rounds was getting your day off to a good start by doing what the Hopi Indians used to do. Rising at four a.m., facing the east, taking all your clothes off and then 'washing yourself in the rays of the sun'. A good day guaranteed – you'll get the part, you won't feel hungry, whatever is your heart's desire. And I wouldn't be surprised if this notion rocks up on our shores sooner or later (although people will have their work cut out to find any sun rays to wash themselves in, but however).

So why, in holy Catholic Ireland, where we're sorted for divine love and eternal life, are people talking about 'positive energy', hanging dream-catchers from their windows and consulting the I-Ching?

There are a variety of theories – apparently, the end of a

century is a time when people traditionally go bananas. The last decade of the nineteenth century was called the Naughty Nineties on account of folk losing the run of themselves. And as for the end of a millennium, well, all hell breaks loose entirely . . . At the end of the last one many people assumed the world was going to end. Likewise with this one. Even though the date from when the two thousand years began running is entirely arbitrary, some are convinced that it *means something*.

As well as millennium fever, there are other reasons for so much alternative spirituality knocking around. The eighties in Ireland were economically depressed, but in Britain, where I lived, things were booming. Money mattered, the labels on your clothes were vital and the size of your flat was an indication of your worth as a person. Altruism was for wimps. You stepped over the homeless person and scorned the disadvantaged because you were eating black-squid-ink pasta and buying three-hundred-quid jumpers from Joseph. What did you care? Money was spent, spent, spent, being poured into the hole at the centre of one's psyche in an attempt to plug it.

Though not everyone was a junk-bond trader, so many aspired to be. But there came a certain point where the expending of cash just wasn't hitting the spot. No matter how many British Telecom shares people owned, they still didn't feel content. Hopes were high that their new Golf GTi would finally fix them, that their next Club Med holiday would do the trick, that all they needed was to up the number of black-squid-ink-pasta dinners they had.

But most sociological patterns are cyclical and the eventual reaction to extreme materialism and its commensurate hang-over is to look for a spiritual element to things. (A bit like swearing you'll never drink again after a hard night on the sauce.) Around the start of the nineties in London, there was an upsurge of interest in a form of Buddhism. The form, unfortunately, where you chant for money and possessions, but Rome wasn't built in a day. A loaded young stockbroker friend moaned to me that he needed to get back to basics, to rediscover what was important. To that end he was taking himself and his £100,000 Porsche on a random drive across Europe, and as a nod to his new hairshirt-and-ashes existence, he proposed driving in his bare feet.

It was around then that the first whisperings of the healing quality of crystals began. Basically, you bought a load of crystals, placed them at regular intervals around your matt-black flat and waited to stop feeling like shit. Shortly after that, meditation as a commodity made its appearance. You gave a ton of money to someone who'd been to India and they taught you to repeat a word over and over again and thereby achieve peace of mind.

Naturally enough, alternative spirituality crossed the Irish sea – sooner or later most British social phenomena make their way to Ireland (except maybe Paddy-bashing). Also, we're in a very strange position in Ireland at the moment: the stranglehold the Catholic Church had on this country has largely disappeared, but a vacuum has been left by its departure. No matter how sophisticated human beings become, it seems that the need to know there's something 'out there' is relentless. To have faith in something, to be happy – that's what most people want, isn't it? (With the possible exception of Leonard Cohen.) So into this vacuum has rushed all manner of codology.

Which I'm very drawn to – always have been. I'm madly superstitious, and I love having my fortune told. (Which sends my mammy wild with annoyance. 'They're only a crowd of money-grabbing charlatans,' she exclaims. 'Wouldn't it be more in your mind to pray to the Holy Spirit?') In my time I've consulted Angel Divination cards, burnt wish-kit candles and tried to read Ogham sticks. But I've learnt something. There's no point having crystals in my sitting-room if I step over hungry, homeless people on the streets of Dublin, if I refuse to buy *The Big Issues* from Bosnian refugees, if I turn away people in need or if I deliberately cause someone harm with my actions or words. I can *fill* the room with crystals and I'm still going to feel like shit.

I didn't have a lot of time for the Catholic form of codology, but I'd liked one of the things that that Jesus bloke said – do unto others as you would be done by. Now, *there's* a thought for the new millennium.

First published in *Irish Tatler*, November 1999.

FRIENDS AND FAMILY

As you will be hearing a lot about my family in this section, I'll give a little bit of info. Like most people, I was born; but unlike most people, I was born a month late. The net result was that instead of being a sunny, dynamic Leo, I am a neurotic, nit-picking Virgo (or maybe it's just me). It was a hard lesson and since then, I always try to arrive on time.

Like many people, I have a set of parents, a mother and father, one of each. They are very nice and decent. I'm sure I've been a great trial to them, what with having first been a teenager, then an alcoholic. But they are so nice that whenever anyone says to them, 'You must be very proud of Marian' (i.e., she gave up the sauce and managed to get published), they invariably reply, 'We were always proud of her.' See what I mean – decent! They are called Ted and Mary. Ted was an accountant, now retired. He knows everything there is to know about women's fiction and regularly rearranges the displays in the local bookshop so that the only books you can see – floor to ceiling – are mine. Mary – popularly known as Mam even to people who aren't her children – is the best storyteller I have ever met. I'm always on at her to write a book, and maybe she will one day.

I am the eldest of five. Many of my siblings have been decent enough to move abroad so that we have nice places to go on our holidays. Niall is three years younger than me and lives in Prague. He is married to Ljiljana and they have a little girl called Ema. She is the world's cleverest, most beautiful child. Caitríona is four years younger than me and lives in New York. Tadhg and Rita-Anne are twins, eight years younger than me. Tadhg is trying to decide where to live — I have respectfully suggested the Maldives. Rita-Anne lives in Dublin and is resisting any pressure to move. Despite this I am still very fond of her. In fact, I am very fond of them all.

I am married to a man called Himself (he also answers to the name of Tony). I met him in England and have imported him to Ireland. He's calm and easygoing, except when his football team are doing badly.

Till Debt Us Do Part

This was written for Image *about a year after I got married, while I was still coming to terms with what it meant . . .*

When I got married at the age of thirty-two, I expected some changes in my life. Naturally, I was prepared for some feelings of loss to accompany the huge realization that for as long as I lived I would never, ever again have another boyfriend. Ever.

Ever again. I mean, NEVER.

But I didn't expect the day-to-day stuff to change very much. After all, Himself and I had done the economically viable thing and lived together for a few months before walking up the aisle. (It wasn't just economics, it was actually a question of survival – my flat in Notting Hill was so cold in the winter I had to put my coat on before going to bed, so I like to joke that I'd have moved in with any man who had central heating. But anyway.)

So I thought we knew each other. He had seen me without make-up. I had seen his Santa Claus underpants. I knew about the Genesis belt buckle he had. He had tried to eat a meal I had cooked (I use the word very loosely). I had seen photographs of him snogging other girls. He had seen the picture of me making my confirmation.

I didn't think we had anything left to surprise each other with. I thought we were safe.

But, suddenly, almost from the second we were pronounced man and appendage, he decided I had become Wife, Great Finder of Things.

It began almost immediately. One morning a couple of days after we got back from honeymoon, I was shaken awake by Himself, who was getting ready to go to work. 'Author Girl, Author Girl,' he hissed. 'Author Girl, wake up.'

'Wha'?' I asked, hair sticking up all over the place, my eyes slitty with sleep.

'Do you know where my cufflinks are?' he asked.

'What time is it?' I mumbled.

'Seven o'clock. Have you seen my cufflinks?'

'Cufflinks?' I muttered, in a daze. 'How would I know where your cufflinks are? I didn't even know you *had* cufflinks, now let me go back to sleep.'

To the sound of him tearing a drawer apart, I pulled the duvet back over my head, talking quietly to myself. 'Don't know what's wrong with him . . . cufflinks . . . middle of the bloody night . . . did you ever? . . .'

And when I woke up again, I thought I had dreamt the whole thing. At least I hoped I had.

So imagine my alarm when, a couple of evenings later, he spent about an hour and a half banging and rooting around in a cupboard in the kitchen. Then he marched into the front room – obviously in a right fouler – and said accusingly, 'Where's my metal tape measure?'

There and then I decided to grasp the nettle, swallow the medicine and address the issue. He had obviously read some sort of 'How to be a Husband' manual and it was time to put a stop to it. 'Now look here,' I said. 'I know nothing of metal tape measures. I am, after all, only a woman. And you're to stop asking me to find things for you. I haven't been visited with psychic powers since we got married.'

'Hah!' he said, throwing his head back. 'Hah!'

'Hah, what?' I asked nervously.

'Hah!' he said again. 'That's good coming from the woman who had me crawling around on my hands and knees . . . on my hands and knees looking under the couch for her glasses, for a good thirty minutes . . .'

'Oh that,' I murmured.

'. . . when all the time she had them on her head.'

He folded his arms and nodded at me self-righteously. 'There's a pair of us in it, you know.'

'That was a one-off,' I protested.

'Is that right?' he said, suddenly very sure of himself. 'What about every time we're just about to go out and we have the obligatory panic looking for your bag?'

I hung my head.

'Well?' he asked. 'Maybe it's upstairs in the bedroom, you say, and I say, When did you last see it? And you say, I can't remember. And I talk you back through it and you eventually remember you had it in the kitchen. So do you know who always finds it? Me!'

'OK,' I admitted. 'You're right. I suppose this is what they mean when they say you have to work at marriage. We must both try harder to find our own things.'

'No,' he said. 'We're married, we're allowed to ask the other person to help us find things.'

I was suddenly very taken with that idea.

'Right, I get you,' I said. 'That's what they mean when they say marriage is a partnership.'

'Exactly.'

And it's not just the dynamic between the two of us that has changed. How the outside world perceives me is also different. Shortly after we got married, I rang him at work and a man's voice said, 'Who's calling? Is that his wife?'

My first instinct was to splutter, 'His what? You mean he's married? The dirty louser and he never told me. I never even suspected!' Until I realized, with a shock, it was *me* the man was talking about. 'Er, yes,' I grinned coyly. 'I suppose, now that you mention it, it *is* his wife.'

And it took me about six months before I could say the words 'my' and 'husband' one after the other, without becoming slightly hysterical with laughter. It just struck me as a ridiculous thing to do. Saying 'my husband' felt like the emotional equivalent of dressing up in my mother's clothes and shoes when I was a little girl. Fun to do, but I was fooling no one.

Then, the whole financial aspect of being married is very

weird. Obviously, when we got married, we – in theory, at least – merged both our properties. There was a part in the ceremony when we gave each other a little silver yoke and said, 'Accept this little silver yoke, a token of all I possess.' (Except when it came to my turn, I had to say, 'Accept this little silver yoke, *all* I possess,' because of my shocking skintness.) But while it's very easy to preach joint ownership in the abstract, in practice it's very difficult to cease being a fully self-supporting, self-governing autonomous monetary unit (in his case) or a human third-world country (in mine). It took a while for me to realize that as soon as I'd paid back one bank loan, it was no longer automatic to immediately apply for another.

At first it was hard to break the habit of being financially independent. Doing the weekly shop was initially a minefield. We took it in turns to pay, me one week, him the next. And I used to get into a right yoomer whenever I felt that too many luxury goods were being purchased the week I had to pay. 'Look at him,' I'd think bitterly. 'Firing family-sized packs of caviar into the trolley just because it's my turn. And next week, when it's his turn to cough up, we'll be lucky to get away with a couple of dented cans of peas.'

Until he reminded me that it actually doesn't make any difference who pays for what. And that if I'm skint he's happy to pay. He's a very sensible, kind, patient man. And I finally think I'm getting the hang of this being married lark. We hardly ever argue – properly argue, as opposed to having stimulating, thought-provoking discussions about cufflinks and handbags. But the great thing is that when we do argue, we have very flexible boundaries within which to have the row – they'll stretch, but won't break. I like the feeling that we'll both stick around to make sure it works.

Mind you, now and then he still makes unusual requests of me.

Like, one day he just turned round to me and out of the blue said, 'Have you any stamps?'

'Me?' I looked around to see was there anyone else in the room he might be talking to. Because he surely couldn't have meant me. 'Why would I have stamps? You know me. You know how disorganized I am. I pride myself on it.'

'I just thought you might,' he said moodily. 'In your purse.'

'Tell me,' I said confidentially. 'Did your mother always carry stamps in her purse?'

'Maybe,' he said sullenly.

'Well, I'm not your mother,' I said matter-of-factly. 'Now, any chance of a lift into town?'

'And I'm not your father,' he replied. 'Make your own bloody way.'

First published in *Image* magazine, March 1997.

You Can Run But You Can't Hide

I have a friend called Jenny. We've known each other a very long time, but since I moved back to live in Ireland we don't see each other often. Recently I went to visit her in London and when I let myself in with the key she'd left out for me, I found her on the floor of her front room doing sit-ups. 'Hiya,' she called. 'Just another sixty of these and I'll be with you.'

'Fine,' I replied, easily. 'I'll just . . .' I looked around for entertainment and spotted something interesting. 'I'll just read your credit-card bill.'

That's because Jenny is a Long-Term Friend. Someone I've known for so long that we don't have to bother with any social niceties – like good manners!

I only have a couple of LTFs: Jenny, who I've known since my teens, and Suzanne, who I've known since childhood. Suzanne also lives in London and I stayed with her about four months ago. Sometimes, other friends who haven't seen me for a while make my arrival a major deal: they clean their flats, they cook meals, sometimes they even get the camera out and take photos. But Suzanne treats me as an extension of herself, we're just straight in, exactly as it always was. There's no awkwardness, no warm-up period, and no special treat-ment. Not only was her flat in a shambles (her own word), but she'd had no time to get any food in and the minute I was in the door I had to help her kill a bee that was marauding around her bathroom. No sooner was that done than she had to go to the post-office and the dry-cleaners, so I tagged along. Errand-running doesn't belong in some friendships, but it does in this kind. There's a real comfort in the ordinariness and timelessness of it.

There are certain other characteristics that mark Long-Term Friendships as different to ones that you might have made when you were slightly older. For example, when I meet people on a social basis, I kiss them. It's what's expected, it's what you *do*. But Suzanne and I can't kiss each other – we just feel too stupid. Our friendship was cemented in the days when the customary form of greeting was to trip each other up or to administer a 'dead arm' – a powerful blow to the vaccination part of our upper arm. Kissing was simply a ridiculous cringy activity for film stars or grown-ups. Then, overnight, the world changed and we found our-selves in our twenties and suddenly, left, right and centre, people were planting sophisticated kisses on each other's cheeks. Not to be found lacking in social graces, Suzanne and I rose to the occasion, and now we can work our way through a roomful of people, kissing as we go. Until we get to each other, then we hesitate, pull back, shake our heads and go, 'Naaaaah!' Then she tries to trip me up and I punch the top of her arm and – greetings having been formally exchanged – we move on to the next person, our lips puckered.

Birthday presents are another area where a Long-Term Friendship is different to an ordinary one. With most friends, when your birthday is approaching, you can hint – heavily even – at what you'd like. But if you don't like what you're given, you pretend you do, because it's the thought that counts, right? But with your LTF, there's none of that altruism. They corner you and say, 'Now look, I have to talk to you about my birthday present. We don't want a repeat of what happened when I was twelve.' And you bow your head and cringe at the memory of giving a twelve-year-old a jewellery kit that the box said was suitable for eight to eleven-year-olds. And it wasn't even your fault because your mother had picked it.

'Think Mac,' your LTF advises. 'Think lipstick.'

'What colour?'

'*This* colour,' she announces, pulling a lipstick from her bag and giving it to you. 'You owe me fifteen quid.'

Having a LTF makes for wonderful reminiscences – well, a different class of them, anyway. With other people, I remember old boyfriends, wild parties, the glorious summer of '95, the shopping trip when we realized that flares were on the way back, the day we first used the word 'partner' to describe our blokes. But when Suzanne and I wander down memory lane, the conversation is more likely to go, 'Do you remember the day we nearly drowned at Laragh?'

''Course I do. I was nine, wasn't I?'

'And your dad went mental.'

'And so did yours.'

'God, the laugh we had!'

But the downside with LTFs is that you can get away with less. They know your patterns, so there's nowhere to run to, nowhere to hide. Many's the time when I've made a dog's dinner of my life, and tried to lessen the mortification and self-loathing by insisting, 'This is the first time this has ever happened to me.' Like it's not my fault, you know? Like it's just an unfortunate accident. And if someone hasn't known me very long, they'll believe me and rain down soothing sympathy, and lo and behold, I get the desired response and feel better. But it doesn't happen with your LTFs. For example, when I got bollocked for being late for work, I complained at bitter length to Suzanne that I was actually a very punctual person and that I was nearly always *early*, and how unfair it all was, and anytime she wanted to join in and say how unfair it was too was fine with me. But instead of heaping scorn on my boss, she furrowed her brow ominously, then effortlessly retrieved a memory from sixteen years ago. 'But what about the time you used to babysit for the Cartys? D'you 'member? You were so late that Mrs Carty had to get her sister to come instead and you were given the boot. D'you 'member? You were late for work then, too.'

'That was different,' I muttered.

But I suppose it wasn't. These friends have the large-scale

map of who we really are. Which can sometimes be a right pain and, more often, can be strangely comforting . . .

Previously unpublished.

Bah! Givvus a Humbug

I got married at Christmas. Not actually on the twenty-fifth of December, but four days later – in other words, as near as made no difference. It was one of those things that seemed like a good idea at the time. I was living in London, but getting married in Dublin, and a lot of people who were invited to the wedding were also living in London, but being ex-pats would be in Ireland over Christmas, partaking of the seasonal festivities with their families and ideally placed for a spot of wedding attendance. But what I hadn't realized was that having a wedding at Christmas would have some unwelcome side-effects. And basically, what happened that year was that Christmas got cancelled in our house. The family diet had started six months earlier. I was home from London for the weekend and half-noticed that the dinner portions served up by my mother were sparser than the gargantuan spreads she usually produced. But it was when the meat and two veg were finished and the time for dessert rolled around that I noticed how bad things had got. Instead of flinging wide the freezer-door, like he always did, and shouting temptingly, 'Magnum? Brunch? Wibbly Wobbly Wonder?', my father switched on the kettle to make tea.

'What's going on?' I asked. There was a chance, admittedly small, that they hadn't been to the freezer centre and were currently out of their stockpile of ice-creams, but in that case why hadn't they offered me bananas and custard?

'We're on a diet,' my mother informed me. 'I'm not having us looking like Billy and Bessie Bunter in your wedding photographs. We have to live with those images for all eternity, so we're going to be fine and thin for them.'

I stared at my father. Was it true? He had a healthy fondness for confectionery, surely he wouldn't give in without a fight. But he just nodded sadly, like a broken man. 'We don't want to look like Billy and Bessie Bunter,' he repeated, obviously brainwashed.

With creeping foreboding, I clocked the warning signs. How could I not have noticed earlier? A carton of low-fat milk on the table. A tub of polyunsaturated spread by the bread. Horrified, I went to the high cupboard and opened it, desperate to be brained by the usual avalanche of Hobnobs, Jaffa Cakes, Boasters and Clubmilks. But nothing fell on to my head except some anaemic crumbs, which obviously belonged to some 33-per-cent-fat-reduced digestives.

So it was true.

And every weekend I came home after that it remained the same. My mother, a gentle and kind-hearted woman, can be a fairly formidable prospect once she gets the bit between her teeth. Rumours reached me – never confirmed, mind – that a Wagon-Wheel wrapper had been found in my father's coat pocket. The implication being that he'd cracked under the low-fat regime in the homestead and had started playing away. But like I said, it was never confirmed.

Anyway, Wagon-Wheels or no Wagon-Wheels, by the time Christmas rolled around, everyone was looking pretty svelte.

I don't know what kind of madness had overtaken me, but I thought that my mother would declare an armistice on the family diet for Christmas Day at least. Most Christmases you can hardly squeeze yourself into my parents' house for boxes of biscuits, chocolates, twelve-packs of chip sticks, acres of cans of Budweiser and one pineapple. They are generous and convivial hosts. My father is a blur, as he marches between the boot of the car and the dining-room, heaving in yet another stack of biscuit tins, just one more armload of mixers. Traditionally, my mother surveys the mini off-licence in the sitting-room and says anxiously, 'But will we have enough? What if someone calls?'

However, this year it was Little-Match-Girl territory: the house seemed bleak, the cupboards seemed bare. (They weren't really, of course, but all these things are relative.) And from the resentful looks my siblings kept shooting me, it was clear who they held responsible for this state of affairs.

'No selection boxes!' Caitríona yelled. 'But how are we going to have the selection-box challenge without selection boxes?' (The selection-box challenge, a game for two or more players, involves eating the contents of a selection box against the clock. An old favourite of mine, and one that I'm actually extremely good at.)

'Play it with apples instead,' my poor father suggested, quailing from the black looks we threw him.

'Christmas is about more than selection boxes,' Mam dared to suggest. More black looks. (If it hadn't been for the industrial-sized tin of Roses that my boss had given me, I don't know *what* I would have barricaded myself into my bedroom with on Christmas Eve.)

Two nights before the wedding, on the twenty-seventh of December, my mother held a do in the house. It was a bonding exercise with Himself's family. As the in-laws are English, my parents felt the full rigours of Irish hospitality weighing heavy on their (by now) slender shoulders. Suddenly all this food and drink appeared from nowhere.

The kitchen table, which hadn't seen much action in the last while, was transformed into a vision of delicious nosh, both savoury and sweet – biscuits, smoked salmon on brown bread, cashew nuts, pastries, quiche, mini-sandwiches and a pineapple. The worktops were a veritable hive of activity, with my father jabbing sticks into cocktail sausages and my mother slicing a Christmas cake that had miraculously materialized.

'Where've you been hiding all this?' Tadhg demanded.

'In the car,' my poor mother said sheepishly. Then she admonished, 'No!' as he tore open a bag of nuts and began to tip them into his mouth, as though drinking from a bottle. 'They're for the visitors!'

'It's the least you can let me have,' he challenged. 'After you've practically STARVED us all Christmas.'

(I digress here, but I'd love to know exactly what triggers grown adults to behave like spoilt brats as soon as they spend more than half an hour under their parents' roof. Even now I can't stop doing it.)

The English visitors duly arrived, and were wheeled into the kitchen to meet my siblings for the first time. Tadhg nodded and beamed with his mouth shut, but didn't actually speak, hindered as he was by the slice of quiche he'd crammed into his mouth but hadn't had time to swallow while Mam had been answering the door.

Throughout the evening, my mother patrolled as much as she could, but she couldn't be everywhere at once and I managed to secrete a box of Chocolate Kimberleys out of the kitchen and spirit them up to my bedroom, where Caitríona and I had a brief but satisfying biscuit-eating frenzy.

The following morning the fear kicked in. The mud-wrap I'd had to slim away the Roses had been worse than useless and I was terrified that my Chocolate-Kimberley orgy had entirely put the mockers on me sliding into my wedding dress.

It was touch and go – the zip was very reluctant to go up all the way. But everything went fine on the day and I have some lovely photos of my mam and dad. They're like stick insects (nearly).

First published in *Irish Tatler*, December 1999.

Himself is a Hooligan

*H*imself likes football. That's because he's a man. I don't like football. That's because I'm a woman. Although I pretend I love it. That's because I'm a *modern* woman.

When Himself declared his interest in the game, it came as a bit of a shock. He's a mild-mannered man with more than a passing fondness for classical music and jazz. And between yourselves and myself, jazz was the thing that I saw as storing up trouble for the future.

I hate jazz and make no bones about it. I just don't get it. I hate the unpredictability of it, all that self-indulgent meandering. What I'd like to know is, where's the chorus? What's wrong with having a rhythm? I want something I can tap my foot to without seeming as if I'm trying to send a message in morse code.

The football problem turned out to be more acute than I'd initially thought. It transpired that he does more than just like football in the abstract. He has a team that he follows and has done since he was a small boy. (Not one of your glamour teams, but a success-challenged crew called Watford.) He goes to their matches, is joyous and ecstatic when they win; moody, sullen and uncommunicative when they don't. He has high hopes that our unconceived son will play for them.

He even buys the crappy merchandise. Their ground is in a place called Vicarage Road and I am the unproud owner of a pair of alarmingly expensive, red, synthetic knickers with the words 'I scored at Vicarage Road' written across the front.

I didn't want to be one of those cardigan-wearing, wifey types who click their tongue and throw their eyes skyward every time football is mentioned. At least I wanted to pretend I wasn't. With a horrible sense of foreboding, I realized I'd have to make a bit of an effort.

Luckily, on account of football being the new rock 'n' roll, I knew the basics when I met him. (Although times have moved on, and now that comedy is the new football maybe the rest of you can all stop faking interest in the sport soon. You lucky articles.) So I already knew that Man United wear red shirts, that Ooh Ah Cantona was probably a worry to his mother, and that the one with his eyes too close together, giving him the aspect of a village idiot, was Ryan Giggs. I understood that I was supposed to fancy him. What I didn't understand was why.

Unfortunately, when Himself talked about football it wasn't the fancyability or otherwise of Ryan Giggs that he wanted to discuss. It was all a lot more technical than that. So I forced myself to learn. I asked questions and managed to listen to the answers without going into a boredom-triggered coma. And now, God love me, I understand the rules. I can bandy about expressions like 'penalty area' and 'we was robbed' with the best of them. I have even been initiated into that innermost sanctum, the holiest of holies, by knowing what the offside rule means.

The only problem is, despite my wealth of knowledge, I still don't like football. The urge to click my tongue and throw my eyes skyward every time it's mentioned is still sore upon me.

After we'd been going with each other a while, he asked me to go to a match with him. 'It's not every girl I'd bring to a match,' he said fondly. I smiled tightly. I agreed to go for three reasons and three reasons only. 1) I loved him. 2) He promised to buy me chips on the walk from the pub to the ground. 3) I was let off having to go and see a jazz saxophonist at Ronnie Scott's, a musician who'd been ominously described as 'a purist'.

And what a revelation that match was. The atmosphere was disconcertingly tribal and primitive. There was so much testosterone in the air that it was a wonder I didn't grow a beard. But worst of all was the change in me laddo – by day a mild-mannered computer analyst, but on Saturday afternoons at football matches . . .

Who *was* this snarling animal beside me, his face contorted with hate, who bellowed tunelessly, 'YOU'RE SHIT AND YOU KNOW YOU ARE' at the faceless supporters at the far end of the pitch? I was horrified. And worse was to come. 'Come on,' he said, elbowing me. 'Why aren't you singing? Join in. You're shiiiit and you know you . . .'

The unpalatable truth is that his team aren't very good.

They're in the first division, which anyone in the know knows is actually the second division. I went to a couple more matches and I was in an agony of frustration because the eejits wouldn't score. They'd get all the way to the net and then they'd hang around shyly, like an adolescent boy trying to pluck up the courage to ask a girl to dance. 'After you,' they cordially invited their team-mates with a flourish. 'No, I insist, after *you*.' Fear of success, I diagnosed.

I put a proposition to Himself. 'Can we support someone else? Someone who wins occasionally?'

He was outraged. He spluttered and stuttered about loyalty and steadfastness, for better or worse, in sickness and in health. 'You can't choose who to support,' he scolded. 'It's something you're born to, it's thrust upon you, you have no say in the matter.'

'It's only a football team,' I muttered. 'Not your destiny.'

'And exactly who were you thinking of switching your allegiance to?' he sneered.

'Well, er . . .' I said, suddenly not so sure of myself. I hadn't been expecting such a violent response. 'I was thinking maybe of Man United . . .'

'Man United!' His face was a picture of disgust. 'That crowd of tossers.' It's really quite astonishing how many people despise Man United and all their works. 'The only people who support them know nothing about football,' he spat. Well, that suited me perfectly.

But the worst thing of all about football is that it gets under your skin. Even when you don't want it to. Even when you fight it. Because the last time I was at a match and 'their' side matched 'ours' in repeatedly failing to kick the ball into the back of the net, I was appalled to find that the person lustily leading the singing, to the tune of *One Packie Bonner*, of '...SCORE IN A BROTHEL, YOU COULDN'T SCORE IN A BROTHEL' was *me*.

First published in *Irish Tatler*, November 1997.

Push!

*U*ntil recently, I knew no one who had a baby. The closest I got was occasionally when a friend of a friend got up the duff. But they were always organized, bossy women who wore Alice bands and yellow cotton trousers, and who seemed to strongly disapprove of me.

'Oh, so-and-so is up the pole,' my friend would say. And I'd murmur some platitude while thinking that – like Formula One engines or the mating habits of humming birds – pregnant women had simply *nothing to do with me*.

But the whole process moved a huge jump closer when *my* friends began having babies. And suddenly the net tightened even further by me becoming so outrageously broody that I'm a danger to myself and others.

I look at a baby and my womb *twangs*. Literally starts lepping around looking for a bit of baby-carrying action. Out of the blue I have empathy with those women who steal babies from prams left outside newsagents. If I pass a pushchair in the street I go all gooey. Starry-eyed, I ask Himself, 'Did you see the beautiful baby?' 'No,' he usually replies, very, very firmly.

My reactions to the idea of pregnancy are mixed. On the

one hand, it'd be lovely to eat for two. Not that I don't anyway, but it would be nice not to feel guilty about it. On the other hand, I've spent my entire life trying to refashion my body into something I can look at without wincing. Pregnancy would put the final kibosh on that dream, because I'm the kind of person who'd put on four stone during the nine months, and never be able to lose them again.

Another impediment to my desire to get pregnant is my dreadful cowardice. I'm baffled why something as allegedly natural as childbirth should hurt so much. Mother Nature must have had an off day – been out on the rip the night before, maybe – when she sat at the drawing-board and invented the ins and outs of giving birth. I mean, it doesn't make sense. It's the biological equivalent of painting oneself into a corner. Yes, Mother Nature, I can see how it gets *in* all right, no complaints there, but you're impressing no one with your plan for getting it back out again.

However, there's a conspiracy of silence around the agony of childbirth. I keep collaring friends who've had babies and begging, 'Be honest with me, be truly honest with me. Tell me how horrific the pain was. I need to know.' And instead of them going into long, gory descriptions, they just smile dreamily and say, 'I suppose it stung a bit. But then when it's all over and you look at the baby in your arms, you think to yourself, A BABY! What a miracle! The day I had Heidi/ Lennox/Saoirse was the first day in my life that I felt whole and complete . . .'

'Does it hurt more than having your legs waxed?' I

brusquely interrupt their lyrical reminiscences. 'Would it make your eyes water?' But they just laugh oddly and never really elaborate.

My friend Kathy is the only person who'll be halfway honest with me. 'Did you ever see a cowboy film, where someone has been caught by the Indians and tied between two wild stallions, each pulling in opposite directions?' she asked.

I nodded mutely.

'That's a bit what giving birth is like. But then you have a baby at the end of it all. A BABY! It's such a miracle . . .'

'Thank you,' I said, moving away to sit down with my head between my knees.

Kathy was the one who was full of talk of having her baby the natural way. She scorned the idea of pethidine because giving birth was going to be the most profoundly powerful experience of her life and she wanted to be fully conscious for it. As for an epidural – she declared loudly and at length that she'd never heard anything as gross as having a needle put into your spine to numb sensation. There was no need for any of that chemical stuff, she said. She was going to give birth in a pool where the water would muffle the pain. And hey, she always had her breathing exercises!

Shortly into her labour, she was begging for gas and air. Which made her puke. Next she beseeched them for some pethidine, which felt like being on a bad trip and did nothing to blunt the pain. Before too long she was roaring for an epidural, but she'd left it too late.

'Breathe!' her fella urged her. 'Come on, remember what we learnt in the class. Deep breaths in, deep breaths out.'

'Eff off!' she sobbed, her face contorted, sweat sluicing from her. 'This is all your fault. If I survive this, and I don't think I will, you're never to come near me with your willie again.'

So you can see my concern. I want an epidural, *at the very least*.

But worse than the fear of giving birth is the fear of *not* giving birth. My friend Judith's baby was so late that she turned to me one day, during her tenth month of pregnancy, and said in a high, tight voice, 'I'm never going to have this baby. I'm going to be pregnant for ever. Until the day I die. But it's OK. I've come to terms with it.'

She was mortified. Each Tuesday she left her prenatal swimming classes, overwhelmed with good wishes as the other women twinkled, 'Don't suppose we'll be seeing *you* next week.' But every time next week rolled around, Judith had to sidle back in, shamefacedly still pregnant. 'Not yet,' she muttered. In the end she stopped going.

Whenever she and her man, Danny, got into their car, the citizens of their road rushed out to wish them well, mouthing 'Good luck' from their doorsteps, giving her the thumbs-up from their windows, only to be told repeatedly, 'Er, no, we're only going to Tesco.'

Then she and Danny tried to fool Fate by going away for the night to a flash hotel, on the principle that because they'd spent a lot of money and were looking forward to it, something was bound to happen to ruin it. But Fate is no eejit and the evening passed without incident.

Eventually she had the baby, nearly four weeks late.

'What was it like?' I asked, anxiously. 'Was the pain disgusting?'

'I can't remember,' she said, serenely. 'Maybe it hurt a bit. But then I took one look at the baby in my arms and I thought, A BABY! It's such a miracle . . .'

First published in *Irish Tatler*, August 1998.

Rapunzel, Rapunzel, Throw Down Your Hair-Dryer!

*I*n June, a couple of years ago, my brother Niall got married, and as he was living and working in Prague, he had the decency to have his wedding there. Off we went, dozens of friends and family, for a five-day knees-up, flying first to London and then on to the Czech Republic.

The wedding party took up about twenty rows of the plane, and as we Irish have a reputation for being high-spirited yet congenial (in other words we get pissed but we don't start fights), we set about proving it before we'd even left Dublin. There seemed to be a competition on to have a conversation with the person furthest away from you — lots of standing up and shouting over heads, and the trading of obscure insults that goes on between people who've been friends for a very long time. I felt so sorry for the one or two passengers on the plane who weren't in our gang.

We had our first casualty at Heathrow. Not — you'll find this hard to credit — as a result of the drink, but because a member of the party had forgotten his passport. He hadn't a hope of getting on the flight without it so we sadly waved him goodbye.

My mother, my sister Rita-Anne and I had all bought

enormous fragile hats for the shindig. 'Guard them with your lives,' the girl in the hat shop had warned us darkly. 'The smallest bang will knock them out of shape and, whatever you do, don't check them in on the plane. The baggage handlers will take one look at the hatboxes and think, "Posh cows." They'll fire them all over the place and the hats will be in bits by the time you arrive in Peru.'

'Prague,' I'd said absently, and swallowed nervously. I wasn't sure where she was getting her bleak world-vision from, but she'd put the fear of God in us. So we brought our hatboxes on the plane, our arms cradled protectively around them. There was a vicious tug-of-war when an air hostess tried to wrest the box from my mother's hands and put it in the overhead locker, but the poor woman didn't stand a chance. The air hostess, I mean.

By the time we got to Heathrow, trawling around the duty-free holding our hatboxes with the same tenderness you'd afford a container of nitroglycerine was beginning to wear. And I was getting tired of people nudging and sniggering as we passed. 'Here they are again. Those ones with the hats.'

So, having impressed upon him how unbelievably, unbearably fragile they were, we left the precious cargo in the care of my father and off we went to let my mother have a good tut-tut at the cost of La Prairie products. Eventually, we got back to find the hatboxes thrown on top of each other in a higgledy-piggledy pile, with my father's legs stretched out, resting comfortably on the top box. Mayhem ensued.

Some hours later, we arrived *en masse* at the hotel, which was a small, charming marvel of inefficiency. As soon as we'd got to our room I wanted to know if Caitríona had arrived from New York, so I rang Peter, the check-in clerk (also the barman, porter, and chambermaid), who consulted the book and told me that Ms Keyes could be located in room 203. Joyously, I burst into the corridor in my haste to see Caitríona, but skidded to a confused halt when I realized that *my* room was number 203. Back on to Peter to explain the misunder-standing. He apologized profusely and told me Caitríona was in room 405. Up the stairs I belted, but when I knocked on room 405's door it was opened by my mother, standing in her slip. '*What?*' she demanded. 'What are you looking at?'

'I'd like to know what you're doing in Caitríona's room in your slip?'

'This is *my* room,' she said defensively. 'But your father's been up and down the stairs with his bad hip looking for Caitríona, and so far he's only found Tadhg and Rita-Anne.'

Back on to Peter. 'Peter,' sez I. 'There's more than one Keyes staying here. In fact, there's at least seven.'

Later than evening, we had our second casualty – when someone went to pay for a round of drinks at the James Joyce and discovered that instead of the required Czech Crowns he had a walletful of Icelandic Crowns. 'I *thought* I'd got a surprisingly good rate of exchange,' he lamented. 'I should have known.'

We had a couple of days before the actual ceremony, which we spent sightseeing, many electing to do theirs from a barstool in the James Joyce. Everyone goes into spasm about the beauty of Prague, which is indeed so pretty it's barely believable. It looks like a Disneyfied version of a MittelEuropean city, all pastel, pointy-roofed, gingerbread houses, fairy-tale castles and gilded palaces. But what fascinated me most were the Praguish women, as they catch up after fifty years of grey, drab communism – at the moment they've reached about 1985. Big hair, awe-inspiring quantities of make-up, and the more revealing the clothes, the better. It was a man's paradise. The one waitress at our hotel went about her duties almost naked, her slender neck wobbling from the weight of so much orange foundation and purple eye-shadow and Prince Char-*ming* stripes of bright-pink blusher.

She developed a bit of a fondness for Himself, which surprised me, because when you're married you get used to no one flirting with you or your fella, not even each other. Wreathed in smiles, she was, every time she clapped eyes on him. While she made no secret of her contempt for me, with my tinted moisturizer and nude lip-gloss and loose, unsexy – I call them comfortable – clothes. *They're fashionable in Ireland*, I wanted to tell her. *Ever heard of casual chic? Eh?* I could just imagine her complaining to her friends about me – 'I mean,' (in Czech, of course) 'I mean, what does he *see* in her? I wouldn't mind if she made a bit of an effort once in a while.'

The morning of the wedding dawned and it turned out to be the hottest day for fifty years. My father fingered his top hat and morning suit and looked like he was about to cry. 'I'll melt,' he complained.

'Tough,' replied my mother.

Meanwhile, another drama was unfolding. It turned out that there was only one hair-dryer in the entire hotel, but no one could get to it because the girl who owned it had been – accidentally, he insists – locked in her room by her husband. A cluster of desperate women with wet hair gathered in the stone courtyard, four floors under her window, beseeching, 'Rapunzel, Rapunzel, throw down your hair-dryer.'

'No,' she replied. 'It'll smash.'

Eventually we were all ready and the taxis arrived. My driver didn't know the way to the church, so he told me he'd follow one of the other taxis. Which he did *by going in front*. This alarmed me, because I don't want the Czech Republic going round thinking it can usurp Ireland's position as Europe's most illogical and charmingly quirky country.

We got to the church in time. Our hair was dry, our hats weren't bashed, the bride looked beautiful, the groom was handsome, the vows made me cry, the speeches were hilarious, the dancing energetic. A great day.

First published in *Irish Tatler*, June 1999.

Lucky O'Leary: a Prince among Dogs

*T*here are people who love dogs and people who don't. I fall into the latter category and it's not so much that I don't like dogs as that I'm very, very afraid of them. It didn't help that when I was in London I lived near an estate where a pit bull was as *de rigueur* as a criminal record. Every time I left my flat to buy a paper, the place was overrun with tattooed thugs (and that was just the women), sporting evil, stocky dogs as they would a new plastic Adidas jacket. To them the dog was a lifestyle accessory. A statement. (Roughly translated, it says, 'I couldn't afford an Uzi.') These people weren't dog-lovers; they were misanthropes, who never moved aside on the footpath as they lumbered towards me, their gait and the gait of their pit bull exactly matched. All short, bulky limbs, steroid aggression and a kind of side-to-side menacing.

But I'm even frightened of nice dogs, which is a problem if I'm going to visit people who own one. The thought of their dog jumping up on me and – God forbid – *licking* me makes me feel faint with terror. The first time Himself invited me to visit his parents, I was racked with fear. And not just because of the obvious trauma of the In-Law Inspection. But because I discovered they owned a dog that they loved very, very much.

Nervously, I pointed out to Himself that the dog might constitute a problem. So he went and made a few phone calls and came back, all smiles, promising me, 'Everything's taken care of, they've a kennel.' I was overjoyed with relief. Until I realized that perhaps I'd misunderstood. Could it be that *I* might be the one to be chained in the kennel, lapping water from a bowl, howling at the moon, while the dog sat next to my intended on the couch in the good room, his legs crossed daintily, making polite conversation, sipping Lapsang Souchong from a bone-china cup, his little finger crooked?

It's not that I fear being savaged by a dog – well, actually I *do*. But as well as that I'm just terrified of the sheer 'dogginess' of dogs. If I tell you that simply looking at a picture of a dog makes my skin crawl you'll probably have a good laugh at me, but it's the truth.

Life as a dog-fearer isn't easy. Most dog-owners simply insist that I just haven't met the right dog yet. They simply cannot countenance someone not being gaga with adoration for their hound. It doesn't matter how many times I say to them that I've nothing against their canine friend, but that I'm in the grip of an irrational fear. They always nod sympathetically and make soothing noises, and when I've finished outlining my phobia, there's a little pause. And then they open their mouth and say, 'Fair enough, but why don't you just pat Rover/Saddam/Dana/Rebel? Go on, tickle his tummy, he'll love you for it. I'm telling you he wouldn't hurt a fly. Well, apart from that time he savaged the little girl, of course, but she *was* pulling his tail, normally he's the most placid . . .'

I don't know why I have such a phobia. Maybe a dog shoved its face into my pram when I was a baby and bared its teeth at me. Or maybe it's Acquired Fear (a little knowledge of psychology is a dangerous thing) – because my mother was never very keen on dogs either. Although that didn't stop Niall, Caitríona, Tadhg and Rita-Anne demanding, 'Can we get a dog, Mam? Can we, Mam? Can we?' every day for twenty years. To which my mother's invariable reply was, 'If a dog comes, then I go.' There always followed a short pause while my four siblings consulted each other with inquiring faces and quizzical expressions. The result was unanimous. 'Well, all right then, Mam,' an elected spokesman would say. 'Thanks a million and the best of luck in the outside world.'

But there was one dog that didn't put the fear of bejayzus in me. And that dog was the late great Lucky O'Leary. Lucky O'Leary belonged to a family who lived up the road from our house, but he decided he preferred the cut of the Keyes's gib.

I wasn't frightened of Lucky O'Leary because I never really believed he was a dog. I was certain that in a heinous prince-into-frog-type scenario, Lucky O'Leary was a human being who'd had a spell put on him. Except instead of being turned into a frog he'd been turned into a cocker spaniel with ears like a spiral perm.

Strange things happened around Lucky O'Leary. For instance, the front-doorbell of our house was at least five feet off the ground – so high, *I* could barely reach it. Often the bell would ring, but when you went to answer it, the only person there was a two-foot-high Lucky, panting and wagging his tail. 'Howya,' he seemed to say, his ringlets swinging. 'Are you coming out for a bit of a laugh?'

And one afternoon I was in bed with the 'flu. As I lay there aching and sweating I heard this strange, faraway whining. A kind of ghostly, unearthly keening. I was delighted. If I was having audio hallucinations, then I was obviously very sick *indeed* and could look forward to at least another week off school.

For a couple of hours I was quite transported and hummed along aimlessly with the faint howling. Could it be a banshee doing her thing, announcing my imminent death, I wondered dreamily? Through my open bedroom door, I saw my mother trudging up the stairs loaded down with a burden of fresh ironing. Weakly, I tried to explain to her about the banshee and that I needed a pen and paper to write my will. 'In a minute,' she said, indicating the ironing, and she opened her bedroom door. What happened next has never left me.

There was a screeching, yelping cacophany of hysterical relief and Lucky O'Leary shot forth from my mother's bed-room, a blur of doggy fur. Before my delirious eyes he stood on his hind legs, held paws with my mother and danced around in a joyous circle to celebrate his liberation, his curly ears bouncing, ironed shirts and towels flung to the four corners of the landing.

When he'd finished his dance of freedom, he marched up

to me. 'I was *calling* you,' his wounded eyes accused. 'Why didn't you let me out?'

And the strange thing is that from that day to this, no one has been able to explain how Lucky O'Leary managed to get into the house, up the stairs and locked into my parents' bedroom. Stranger still, my mother insists that lots of her make-up had been used and that some of her clothes, shoes and jewellery had been worn . . .

First published in *Irish Tatler*, June 1998.

Now is the Time for All Little Brothers to Come to the Aid of the Party

*H*aving a party – is it a bit like having a baby? Agony at the time, but when it's all over, a strange amnesia kicks in and people can't remember the pain, only the good stuff. Well, that's the only explanation I can find for why I keep having parties.

It was different when I was younger and living in rented flats. Back then shindigs happened smoothly, fluidly, spontaneously. It was simply a question of moving everyone from the pub back to my flat. And what did a cigarette burn or two on the hideous carpet matter – it was probably an *improvement*. And who cared if someone swung on the curtains and half-pulled them off the wall. I could (and did) live with them at half-mast for a good six months (or to put it another way, until I moved out).

Anyway, a while ago I decided to have a party. A *proper* party, with invitations and catered food and what-have-you. So I made a list and was pleasantly surprised to find I knew so many people. Next I constructed an invite on the computer, sent it out and started deciding how much drink and food to buy. I even – more fool me – started to get excited.

But over the next two weeks I got an alarmingly high

number of refusals – people going on holidays or having babies or getting married and all sorts of other unreasonable excuses. If I heard the words 'Any other weekend and we'd have *loved* to come' once, I heard them a hundred times. And even though the invitation said RSVP, not one person had respondez'ed to say they were coming.

The cold hand of fear began to stroke me and all of a sudden I was sorry I'd ever started this. Then I bumped into an invitee in the street and he said that of *course* he'd be there. He even said he was looking forward to it! I tentatively took it as a good omen and decided to stop feeling like Norman No-Mates. If I hadn't had a definite no, then it meant yes.

And so to purchase the jar!

Being a dyed-in-the-wool Irish person, I asked the man in the off-licence how much drink we'd need for a hundred people (the anticipated number of guests). And when he told me, I said, 'OK! Double it!'

'Double it?' Himself asked anxiously.

'No! You're right! Triple it!'

Next, the food. We'd decided on canapés because we didn't feel able to cope with plates: no point trying to run before we could walk. But the cost came as a big shock. 'No, no, I'm talking about *mini*-quiches,' I explained to the girl, thinking she'd misunderstood my request. 'Not full-size ones.' But there had been no misunderstanding and I was baffled as to how they could cost so much. I mean, they're *tiny*. *Mini*, actually – the clue is in the name. Besides, no one eats them:

instead they throw them at people they fancy, then grind them into the carpet when the object of their desire spurns them.

But we bit the bullet and paid up.

In the final week before the big night, the cancellations continued to pour in. I was in the horrors at the thought of no one, *no one at all* turning up. I started going through old Filofaxes and ringing long-disconnected numbers or having conversations that went, 'So he's moved to Argentina? Six years ago? Doesn't time fly? Anyway, I don't know you, but you sound nice – would you like to come to a party on Saturday night? Please.'

In a desperate attempt to people the party with bodies – at this stage I didn't care *who* they were – I rang all my friends and begged them to bring everyone they'd ever met. In a moment of inspiration I told Tadhg – a young man who knows how to enjoy himself – to bring all his friends. He studied me carefully and asked if I knew what I was getting myself into. I assured him that I did. 'Well, on your head be it . . .' he murmured.

The day of the party finally dawned and I took stock: the situation was bad but not unsalvageable. There were still seventeen people from the original list who hadn't cancelled. Tentatively hopeful, myself and Himself went out to collect the food and arrived home to find seventeen last-minute refusals blinking on the answering machine.

It was my darkest hour. I was desperate to cancel the whole horrible, misconceived idea, but couldn't. I looked around at my food-filled kitchen and felt like all the mini-quiches were laughing at me.

The invitation said nine-thirty. On pain of death, my closest friends were there at nine. At a quarter to eleven it was just me, them and the despair. We'd got in a load of Red Squares for the 'young' people, but the thirty-somethings started milling into them with the enthusiasm of the very miserable. Fuelled by vodka and taurine, someone half-heartedly suggested that we could all have a good time anyway. Someone else told her to cop on.

Suddenly, at ten to eleven, the gloomy silence was shattered by the doorbell ringing; it was a man I couldn't even remember inviting, bringing six others with him. Seconds later the bell rang again and it was someone who'd cancelled ('the wedding's off!'), also trailing a small entourage. They made straight for the kitchen and began flinging mini-sesame toasts at each other. I began to relax. This was starting to look like a party.

The bell rang again and when I opened the front door, the garden was filled with a veritable sea of people – Tadhg had arrived, with fifty-seven of his closest friends! I stood on the step feeling like me laddo in the Sermon on the Mount, and welcomed them in. 'The Red Squares are that way,' I pointed. 'Oh, sorry, they seem to be all gone.'

The bell went again. And again. I decided to leave the front door open. I tried to get into the kitchen but couldn't because of the volume of people crammed in there, eating, drinking, laughing their heads off and flicking ash on my wood-laminate floor. In the hall, a girl in a gold lamé halter-top called a girl in a fake Pucci dress 'a minger'. Apparently they were fighting over a dotcom contract. One of the thirty-something Red Square enthusiasts puked. Another one of them had Tadhg in a headlock and was telling him how she'd always fancied him. Things were looking good!

At half-twelve, a neighbour from a few doors up arrived. Funny – I didn't remember inviting him, he was one of the few people in Dublin that I *hadn't* invited. But he hadn't come to partake of the knees-up, he'd come to tell me that he was calling the peelers if I didn't keep the noise down. It was then I *really* relaxed. This party's a hit.

First published in the *Evening Herald*, May 2001.

ALL GROWN UP

Ten Housework Laws for Men

1 Throw away Quentin Crisp's *Guide to Housekeeping*. (Quentin Crisp is the person who famously said that if you stop dusting, the squalor doesn't get any worse after the first four years.)

2 Scrub all empty Cornflakes bowls IMMEDIATELY, before the little bits get the chance to set diamond-hard.

3 Wash the windows – and stop telling us that grimy glass is an economical alternative to blinds.

4 If you're not going to do your own ironing, then be very careful about what clothes you buy – there is a better chance of getting the wrinkles out of a bloodhound's face than out of 100-per-cent-linen shirts.

5 When you finish the Weetabix, put the empty box in the bin – and not back into the cupboard, where it masquerades as food until someone is very, very hungry and very, very disappointed when they discover that it's not.

6 Cooking a delicious meal involves many essential tasks. Making the smoke alarm go off is not one of them.

7 Towels are not as delicate as they look. They can stand being washed more than twice a year.

8 Ditto sheets.

9 Stop pretending that you think that women have an automatic kinship with people who come to the door (milkmen, coalmen, poolsmen, travellers, door-to-door artists, bob-a-jobs, government-training-course drop-outs offering to trim your hedge, escaped criminals, et cetera). You fool no one by standing nervously in the hall shouting towards the shower, 'Er, there's someone at the door – come down, would you? I'd go myself only you're good at this sort of thing. Are you there? Hello?'

10 I don't know *either* where the camera/Nurofen/letter from the insurance is – look for things yourself once in a blue moon. And write a hundred times, 'The womb is not a locating device. The womb is not a locating device. The womb . . .'

First published in the *Irish Independent*, June 1999.

Gilt Trip

Once upon a time, I didn't care. I didn't give a damn. I would no more spend money on the hovel that I inhabited than I would go to a classical concert. My home was a rented flat in London, and it was a haven of hand-me-downs – towels by Mammy, dralon couch by Oxfam, bed by the same person who built Noah's Ark.

And then – seemingly overnight – it all changed. One minute I was refusing to buy any blinds and having to flatten myself against the wall to get dressed without the occupants in the house opposite getting a ringside view of my bits, the next I was weighing up the merits of ash slats versus rice-paper. The momentous day came when I'd only enough space on my credit card to buy a pair of flared-heeled, rubber sandals *or* a three-wicked candle the size of a dinner plate – and the candle won. Truly this was the instant that I crossed into adulthood!

And then I took a look around my flat – and the shock nearly killed me. I couldn't believe I'd ever thought that the Laura Ashley flowery cast-off duvet cover that even my mother didn't want was better than no duvet cover at all. The scales fell from my eyes, I saw the error of my ways and slowly I tried to rebuild my life.

I painted — creams and beiges (with heavy post-modern irony, of course), with the occasional strategic panel of colour. I saved up and purchased: Arne Jacobson kitchen chairs (well, close copies anyway), a glass and chrome coffee table (on sale) and, pride of place, a Loge chair. (I couldn't bring myself to sit in it for the first month, so great was my respect.) I precision-placed: a white vase, a stainless-steel-framed mirror, a lamp made mostly of coat-hangers.

But attempts to put my style-free past behind me and move on with my life were hampered by my relatives. When I told my mother that the so-busy-they-could-trigger-a-fit curtains that she'd palmed off on me were on their way to that great drapers in the sky, she said anxiously, 'But they're good quality. And lined. It would be a shame to waste them.'

Quality? *Quality?* What did quality matter? She was speaking to the woman who was thinking of dumping her boyfriend because he didn't quite go with the dusty grape she'd painted one of her bedroom walls.

'You're obsessed,' said Mammy. Perhaps I was.

But things got worse. My Great Auntie Eileen and Great Uncle Mikey got wind that I was doing up my flat and decided to help. By arriving on my doorstep with a great big lump of a curlicued gilt mirror. 'It was your granny's,' they chorused. 'We'd love you to have it.'

If only there wasn't such a thing as manners. If only I was the type of person who could say, 'Are you out of your mind? It's completely hideous, I wouldn't be able to sleep under the same roof as it.'

Some people can do that – the same kind of mythical people who can downsize their lives. They may, of course, cause a family rift that endures for decades, but what do they care?

Instead I stood aside and let them heft it into the hall.

'Right!' said Great Uncle Mikey, wiping sweat from his brow. 'I'll just get the table.'

Table! There was a table? Yes. A gloomy, mahogany chunk. Apparently it was the first thing they'd bought when they got married, and was steeped in sentimental value.

Too late, I tried protesting that it was very thoughtful of them, but I'd no room.

'Don't be daft,' they said, surveying my (much-laboured-over) light, bright, white, airy space. 'You've nothing here!'

My first instinct was to shove the unwanted furniture in the attic. Except I didn't have an attic. Basement flats usually don't. Then I wondered if I could look on this as an opportunity and *do* something with the invading stuff – other than just chop it up for firewood? Couldn't I paint the table white, perhaps? Although what would happen when Eileen and Mikey called around unexpectedly? I'd have to do some swift scrubbing with methylated spirits to restore it to its original glory(!).

How about hiding the things behind my bendy wooden screen? But I realized wistfully that I'd plans for that screen. Where else was I going to put my (barely used) badminton racket, boots that need heeling, the broken chair (I should have paid the extra for proper Arne Jacobson) and all the other crap I'd been hoping to throw in the corner and mask with the calming blankness of a protective screen?

Luckily, though, we live in fortunate times. Burglars! Where would we be without them? And if you're one of those unlucky few to have been overlooked by the redistributors of wealth, why, you can always pretend! And all I have to live with now is my guilt . . .

First published in *Living etc*, September 1999.

The Agony and the Ecstasy, but Mostly the Agony

A few years ago, I left London and moved back to Ireland, and was having a whale of a time until I realized that everyone was expecting me to behave like an adult and buy somewhere to live. This was written mid-hunt.

For the past five months my life has been acute misery. Living hell. A torment of exquisite anticipations, followed by crushing disappointments. I haven't had a Saturday afternoon to myself since last May. By now you'll surely have deduced that I'm trying to buy somewhere to live. I had hoped that through a combination of eternal youth and acute poverty I'd never have to indulge in this terrible practice – but the gig is up.

I'm a purchase virgin, and while I'd been told that my first time would be painful, nothing prepared me for the extent of the agony.

The drill for the past five months has been as follows: I find a house in the paper that's just about affordable and off I go to see it, and if it's anyway half decent, I want it with a terrible needy desperation borne of the fact that every stick of furniture I own is languishing in a crate in a warehouse on foreign soil. (Himself sold his shoebox in London, and the house we had our eye on in Dublin fell through. I mean, *literally* fell through – the bedroom floor into the kitchen below. Think twice before buying old houses.) Suddenly, all the other people strolling around the property become my mortal enemies. I give them hunted looks and find I'm receiving identical hunted looks in return. The world of house-buying is a dog-eat-dog one and with each property there can be only one winner. With sidelong, anxious glances I try to assess whether they like the place and, more importantly, if they've money or not. I can hardly stop myself from snarling at them, 'Get out, you usurper, this house is *mine*.' Instead, I force myself to murmur in their earshot, 'Christ, what a kip, you'd want to be mad to pay good money for the likes of this.'

Then my mother told me that 90 per cent of people who view houses only go for the crack. They have no intention of buying, they're just there because there's nothing good on telly.

'You can't be serious,' I said. 'What kind of poor, sad eejit spends their spare time doing that?'

'Some people quite enjoy it,' she said, a bit tersely.

This gave me great comfort until the next time we looked. I walked into a bedroom to hear a sleek woman say to her equally sleek fella, 'This could be Sebastian's room and Cressida could have the other one.' Tearfully I turned to Himself. 'We haven't a hope of getting this one. They've got children called Sebastian and Cressida. They must be loaded!'

We've actually gone to auction on a couple of places, and both times we've been pipped at the . . . well, I was going to say *post*. But it's not true. I'd have been delighted if we were pipped at the post. Instead we were pipped before we were even out of the starters' blocks. Outbid by miles, so we didn't even have the consolation of being able to leave the auction room with a 'I coulda been a contender' swagger.

But the real problem with trying to buy somewhere to live is, of course, the estate agents. I hate estate agents. I know I'm probably preaching to the converted here, but I've never had experience of them before, so please humour me. I loathe them with a passionate intensity. Some of the women aren't the worst, in fact one woman called Dorothy is very nice, but I hate the men.

It's not just that they are breathtakingly patronizing, stunningly insincere liars, although of course that helps. It's the fact that men estate agents can't actually see me if I'm not accompanied by a man. I become invisible if I go in the front door of a property on my own. While the spawn of Satan takes other people's details, I loiter, totally ignored. When I try to help myself to a brochure, he absent-mindedly slaps my hand away, the way you would to a small child trying to grab a box of matches. But when Himself appears by my side, after parking the car or whatever, Mr Estate Agent suddenly glides forward, so unctuous he could do himself an injury, greasy paw proffered for the customary dead-fish handshake. 'Have a brochure,' he offers, flicking hard-shark eyes over Himself, trying to gauge his annual income to the nearest fiver.

'It's your one you should really be talking to.' Himself good-humouredly indicates me. 'I'm unemployed, she's the breadwinner.' Mr Estate Agent recoils in horror. Then there's a frantic scrambled attempt to wrest the brochure from the unemployed person's hands – no job, no piece of paper covered in lies – and a hasty attempt to make restitution. 'Well, if your wife would like to . . .'

'I'm not his wife,' I often find myself saying, even though I am.

But last Saturday I suffered the worst indignity to date. The viewing was due to start at two-thirty, but we got there slightly early. We idled in the car for a while, but after I'd searched in the glove compartment and the side pockets and failed to find any sweets, I got tired waiting. 'Come on,' I said at two-twenty-eight, 'We'll chance it.'

But as we advanced up the path, the front door of the house opened and a twelve-year-old in a confirmation suit poked a narky head out and angrily shooed us away. 'We're not ready for you yet,' he shouted.

I turned to Himself. 'The rude little brat,' I gasped. 'I'm going to tell his mother.'

'That's not a child of the house,' Himself said. 'That's Ernest Conner from Patronize and Swizz, the Estate Agents.'

'I don't believe you.' I was stunned. 'I'm not buying a house from someone whose balls haven't dropped yet.'

However, I've learnt a lot from it all. I know now that people really do fall in love with their abusers. Because, despite everything, as soon as Thursday rolls around again there I am, buying the paper to see if the perfect house has miraculously materialized within its pages, then planning my strategy to get round as many places as possible on Saturday . . .

I'll keep you posted.

First published *Irish Tatler*, February 1998.

Scarlet Pimpernel Construction

Finally we got lucky (!)

Some months ago I wrote about moving back to Ireland and trying to buy a house in these heady days of the Celtic Tiger and escalating-before-your-horrified-eyes house prices. Well, Himself and myself finally managed to find a house that we could afford, and it had the added bonus of having the full complement of walls, most of its windows and what would do for a roof until we could afford a new one. Even better, the house managed, by the skin of its teeth, to be in the greater Dublin area, and not – as we'd been resigning ourselves to – in a feeder town a small bit north of Calais.

Would you blame me for expecting the camera to fade out on a roseate picture of me jingling my keys and grinning like a relieved loon? THE END. But it wasn't the end. It was only the beginning . . .

Seconds after the ink had dried on the contract and I was visiting the new house for the first time as *my* house, I finally realized what the term 'north-facing' meant. Of course, I'd previously *tried* to find out. 'What does north-facing imply?' I'd endeavoured to attract the estate agent's attention. 'Hello,

hello . . .' 'Quiet, please,' he eventually hissed at me. 'I'm talking to your husband, man to man.'

But now, as I stood in my new, chilly, funereal front room, gazing in impotent confusion as the sun split the stones outside, I suddenly understood all about 'north-facing.' Just where the boundary of my barely purchased house ended, the air changed from dark-green gloom to drenching, dazzling, yellow light. As every other house in Ireland baked, the sun pouring through all their windows, I shivered and contemplated putting on the heating. Why? I wondered in frantic despair. Why do I always get it wrong? Why does everything I touch turn to crap?

My friend Siobhan tells me this is perfectly normal. 'Oh yes,' she said confidently, when I wept on her shoulder. 'I had that too. It's PPPB – Purchase Post-Partum Blues. You're after tying up every penny you'll earn for the next fifty years in this pile of bricks and mortar. It's natural to have a twinge of doubt. I was pregnant when we bought our house, and every time I walked in there I nearly had a miscarriage.'

'I hate it,' I said bitterly. 'It's like a crypt. I want to sell it immediately, but who'd buy it? A pig in a poke like that. Oh, they saw us coming and no mistake . . .'

'It's grand,' she reassured me. 'You're imagining it.'

Then things got worse, because builders entered into the equation. Scarlet Pimpernel Construction arrived, knocked down a couple of walls, told us we'd rising damp, ordinary damp, dry rot, woodworm, shaky foundations and a dodgy roof, then simply disappeared, more elusive than Shergar.

On the day we were supposed to move in, our house

resembled the scene of a terrible earthquake. Dust and plaster everywhere, concrete walls, yards of wiring, exposed metal pipes skewed at weird angles, water sluicing down walls – barely recognizable as something people once lived in. Aghast, I stood and looked at the wreckage while a sombre voiceover in my head said, 'Hope is running out of finding any more survivors.'

There was no way we could move in – the Red Cross would have arrived to airlift us out of the place. But the lease had ended on our rented flat. Basically, we were homeless. Luckily, my parents very decently let us move in with them, into their lovely (finished) house that had a freezer full of Magnums and a cupboard that strained at the sides with its cargo of Clubmilks.

While Himself turned into a gumshoe, trying to track down the various builders, throwing himself on their mercy, and attempting to get at least one room liveable in, I regressed to childhood. Sleeping in my teenage bedroom, yelling at my mother, 'Is my white top ironed yet? Have you washed my jeans? What crap are we getting for dinner? Not chicken casserole? Awwww! Can't we get McDonald's? Can I have an advance on my pocket money? . . .'

And she was as bad as me. There was a big tussle anytime I tried to wear anything that hadn't been aired for at least twenty-four hours.

'But I never air anything,' I protested.

'While you're under my roof,' she threatened grimly, 'you'll live by my rules.'

'Rub it in, why don't you?' I countered bitterly. 'That you've *got* a roof.'

We stayed with my parents for three weeks and I'd still be there to this day except I'd put on about a stone from all the Clubmilks and Magnums and chicken casseroles and none of my nicely ironed clothes fitted me any more. Meanwhile, the builders had kindly finished one room – the bedroom – so, amidst great trepidation, we moved in.

We'd no kitchen, so all meals were takeaways – nothing new there (I can't cook). Water for the kettle that stood on our bedroom floor had to be fetched from the outdoor tap. Brick dust was omnipresent: in the air, between our bedsheets, behind our eyes. There was no bit of floor intact enough to put our couch on. We seemed to spend a lot of time sitting on our dusty bedroom carpet, eating chips from the local chipper, seasoned with dust, and outdoing each other planning elaborate tortures for the builders. But at least they now showed up – spasmodically, at peculiar hours and without making any kind of obvious progress, but they were definitely there. I couldn't walk out of the bedroom without being wolf-whistled at and hearing, 'Nice pair, darling!'

They were always keen to tell us in elaborate detail why the job was three months late and 100 per cent over budget, but I couldn't bring myself to talk to them. Not because I hated them – although, of course, I did – but because I found the whole thing so tedious. I didn't want to understand any of it, I just wanted it to happen.

But one day Himself had to go out, and he left a list of

things I was to discuss with Eddie the builder when he turned up. 'Don't scare him,' he ordered. 'Try not to act womanly in any way. He's a builder, it makes him nervous.'

'Eddie –' I read from the list: 'The hole beside the fridge is too small. The plug socket can't fit.'

Indisputable.

'Ah, but it has to be that size,' Eddie insisted. 'Do you see this?' – holding up a wire – 'Well, that needs to go through there and with the transformer lined up with the . . .' Off he went, while I faded out and came to, faded out and came to. Words like 'plinth . . . wiring . . . sockets . . . joists . . . kango hammer . . .' floated at me, bounced right off and fell on the floor. There is simply nothing in me for words like that to hook on to. I'm a smooth surface and can't retain them in any way.

So when Himself came back, I was hard put to explain why nothing on the list had got done. 'Eddie, he said . . . words,' I explained miserably, 'and I just couldn't bring myself to care.'

'Ah, now,' he complained. 'We'll never get this place finished!'

And so far he hasn't been proved wrong.

First published in *Irish Tatler*, September 1998.

Get that Dustbin out of my Relationship Corner

*F*eng Shui – sure, haven't I enough to worry about! You can't open a magazine or turn on the radio without hearing all sorts of advice about the relationship sectors and prosperity corners of your home. In China they take it very seriously. On the telly the other day there was a programme about an enormous luxury block of apartments that's just been built in Hong Kong. But there's a huge, gaping hole, the size of four flats, in the middle of it. Not, you may be surprised to hear, as the result of shoddy workmanship, but *put there deliberately*. The reason: so that the 'Ch'i' – that's energy to the likes of you or me – can flow through the hole from the mountains to the town.

Now, under normal circumstances, I'd be an ideal candidate for the whole Feng Shui malarkey – racing out to buy a sackful of wind chimes, painting my front door red or moving my entire flat four degrees to the south as required. I'm very gullible when it comes to signs and portents and presentiments and omens. I love the idea that you can heal your life by doing something outside of yourself. To that end, I have subliminal self-help tapes. I don't listen to them, mind, but I *have* them. I hold with aromatherapy. I know someone who had a chakra healing done and I wanted one too. I've had my aura read and I have plenty of truck with horoscopes and tarot readers.

But with Feng Shui they've just pushed me too far. It's one worry too many in a world where they're always inventing new things for me to fret about. And I usually do my best to obey – I've stopped drinking tap water, I don't go out in the sun without being smothered in Factor Eighty, I feel guilty for drinking fizzy drinks because they allegedly cause cellulite, I don't take my make-up off with toilet paper because it has wood shavings in it, I rarely brush my hair when it's wet and I've stopped my daily asbestos rub.

But I've tried to close my ears and eyes to Feng Shui, because the nightmare that is my new house trundles on (sorry if I'm boring you), and I've enough *tangible* worries concerning it. Like, will the plumber ever come back to fix the shower? Or the fact that the paint looked like a lovely mature shade of clarety red on the chart, but as soon as I'd slapped it on to the shelves, it mutated into Barbie pink. Clashing so badly with the red couch that they go for each other regularly in hand-to-hand combat and have to be separated.

Right now, I've no time, energy or money to deal with *intangible* worries about the house. Hauntings, bad ley-lines, black streams etc. will have to wait a while. Nevertheless, I've managed to pick up enough about Feng Shui to feel very edgy. If I don't want to shag up my life, it's a veritable minefield of dos and don'ts, some of them heavy-duty.

For example, what if my dwelling place faces the wrong way? It'd be an awful lot of work to change my front door to where the back door is, not least because anyone visiting me would have to come via the house-behind-me's yard and over the wall. Also, I have a horrible feeling that the optimum location for a house is beside running water. How am I going to manage that? Until I do, am I doomed to be a miserable failure? It was a happy day, I can tell you, when the men working on the road burst a pipe and water gushed past the gate for a couple of hours. I felt briefly at peace then, like I was doing everything *right*, for once.

I regarded it as a great achievement when I managed to get curtains up in the new bedroom so that the neighbours weren't subjected to the sight of Himself's dangly bits of a morning and driven to choke on their Fruit 'n Fibre. (Even if the curtains were old ones from our flat in London and consequently miles too short, so that they hung at half-mast like a pair of Bay City Rollers trousers.) But my warm glow of homemaking triumph quickly soured when I realized that my husband's modesty may be intact but I still couldn't tell my relationship corner from a hole in the ground.

For all I knew, I could be shaving my legs in that self-same relationship corner. Does that mean Himself will leave me? And I'll have no one to blame except myself? Or what if I inadvertently put my telly in the work corner? Does that mean that I'll spend my days thrun in the bed, watching reruns of *Hart to Hart* and *Hotel*, rather than knuckling down and trying to write a book and thereby putting bread on the table? (Not that I would ever *dream* of spending my time doing such an indulgent, wasteful thing between eighty-thirty a.m. and nine-thirty a.m. and between one p.m. and two p.m. Monday to Friday, except on bank holidays when only *Hart to Hart* is on. God, no!)

And I'm not the only one tormented by anxiety. My friend Ailish had a sleepless night after she heard a Feng Shui expert say that ideally you'd need a pair of ceramic dragons at your front door to guard the house. 'I'm worried,' Ailish confided, 'about where I'll buy the ceramic dragons. Do you think that one of those shops in Temple Bar might have them? Or a garden centre, maybe?'

I can see her point. I've only been in my house-cum-building-site a couple of months and already I've been broken into. But what's wrong with smashing a couple of bottles and sticking the broken bits into Polyfilla along the back wall, if it's guarding you require? Or a 'Beware of the Dog' sign? All too prosaic, I'm afraid. Feng Shui is growing in popularity, and a consultation is almost as much a feature of moving into a new home as a nervous breakdown and a housewarming party.

Will Feng Shui become something for twenty-first-century children to make their parents feel guilty about? Like mothers in the sixties cringing with shame for giving their family shop-bought cake. Will teenagers of the future blame their sense of inadequacy not on the repression of the Church or the strictness of their parents – which was plenty good enough for my generation – but on the fact that their bed was at the wrong angle to the door, thereby 'cutting' good Ch'i?

In the end I had to do something, however tokenistic, to

assuage my Feng Shui anxiety. Slightly sheepishly, I bought a wind chime and hung it by the front door to bring general good fortune to my home. And the next time I came in I forgot it was there and got a belt in the eye that nearly blinded me.

First published in *Irish Tatler*, October 1998.

Too Fast to Live, Too Young to Garden

*G*ardening is the new sex! Well, maybe not, but it's certainly the new something. Once the sole preserve of oul' wans and Protestants, gardening has suddenly achieved popular cachet, and has become – no really, there's no getting away from it – it's become *sexy*.

Out of nowhere, people that I envied for their style, panache, Ghost dresses and thin thighs have begun to enthuse about their 'outdoor room'. So if these style warriors say gardening is groovy, then I suppose it must be.

Perhaps it was inevitable. Interiors were the thing, the new rock 'n' roll or whatever. One minute it seemed that no one gave a damn about the colour of their walls, the next everyone was watching *Changing Rooms* and yearning for a sleigh bed. And now that things have progressed to the point where it's perfectly acceptable for two straight men to have a discussion about which couch they're thinking of buying, maybe the last bastion of fusty adulthood is set to fall.

Hmmmmm. I wasn't convinced. Too fast to live, too young to garden. Tending plants was the most *un* rock 'n' roll thing I could think of.

I had a normal upbringing – there was a smallish patch of

grass at the back of the ancestral family home. Two or three flowers might show their faces every spring, because pollen had been carried on the breeze from someone else's garden, but that was about the size of it. Gardens were places where you hung clothes to dry. Where you stored broken bicycles. And when the rows broke out about the cutting of the grass they became a battleground. You see – perfectly normal! My childhood was idyllically free of talk of 'hardy perennials', 'mulch' or 'bedding plants'. Instead, 'Cut the grass!', 'Cut it yourself!' was the only gardening conversation that took place.

After I left home, I lived for many, many years in a series of grungy flats, where the only amenities that mattered were Fridge, Telly, Bed. If any of the flats had a garden, no one in their right mind would venture into the eight-foot-high grass, for fear of tripping over the rusting, abandoned cars, buried bodies, et cetera left by a succession of equally unconcerned previous tenants.

Then, about a year ago, I bought a house, and the house had a garden. Not that that concerned me initially. I was too interested in the fact that my new home was uninhabitable, thanks to Scarlet Pimpernel Construction, who'd enthusiastically knocked down lots of it, then shagged off before they'd put it back together again.

After several tortuous months, the house was pieced back together. We had a few halcyon days gloriously savouring the novelty of a roof over our heads, convinced we'd never worry about anything ever again. Then, in typical never-satisfied human fashion, we started to paw around for Other

Things to Worry About. Which is where the garden came in.

I got the shock of my life when I realized that the green stuff beyond the window was my responsibility. And that it *grew*. Yes, yes, I know it's elementary. I knew *in theory* that grass got longer, that weeds appeared in flower-beds, that hedges got out of control if they weren't tended. I just never before thought that any of these facts applied to me.

I was genuinely upset. I hadn't time to get my *own* hair cut, never mind deal with a twenty-foot-square version of a head of hair. But there was more to it than that. I just didn't want to be a person who gardened.

I cannot tell you the scorn I used to pour on people who cared about their gardens. They sent me wild with irritation, for reasons that I still find hard to articulate properly. Their stupid gloves, their ridiculous hats and, above all, the odd things they said. To my mind, it was as if they belonged to a cult or had their own secret language when they discussed 'glads' and 'daffs', or cooed hysterically over being allowed to take a cutting from someone else's hedge, or slithered into a pit of gloom because the snails ate their roses. *Cop on, there are people starving!* I always yearned to say.

And one of the worst things that could happen to me was someone offering to show me around their garden. There they'd be, waffling on about this phlox and that sweet pea, lamenting the lack of rain, swooping to pluck greenfly from leaves, like people who brush away imaginary fluff from their clothes. Christ, what a nightmare. *Talk to me about real things!* I wanted to scream. *Connect with me as a human being.*

I found the whole thing repellently anal. And yes, flowers are beautiful. I love flowers. So much so that more than once I've initiated an argument with a loved one, and energetically reapportioned blame, just so I'd get an apology bouquet out of it. But as far as I was concerned, gardening had nothing to do with flowers. Proof positive – you weren't let pick the flowers you grew in your garden. So what was the point?

Because Himself and myself are totally clueless, we tried to find some sort of gardener to try to keep a lid on things, and a friend of a neighbour yielded a plump, angry man who marched into the house and declared, 'I'm no gardener, but I'm a learner. I want a cup of tea every hour on the hour, or else I'm off.' (I'm not making any of this up, I swear.)

I couldn't concentrate on work because I was afraid of forgetting to make his hourly cuppa. Then, every time I took it out to him, he kept me in conversation for thirty minutes, while I became more and more hysterical as work piled up undone. The last straw was when he told me that a certain plant was sage and that I should put it in my stews. Only the fact that I'm as enthusiastic a cook as I am a gardener saved us from being poisoned. Because the plant was lilac.

Wheel on gardener number two, a Canadian, who appeared to be a man of the earth. He certainly *promised* us the earth, definitely *charged* us the earth, then we eventually came *down* to earth when, despite the wedge we'd handed over for bulbs, spring yielded about ten daffodils. Talk about feeling like an eejit!

Gardener number three was very keen. At least, we think he was – we never actually met him. He kept promising to come, but after about a hundred phone calls there was still no sign of him.

Gardener number four, all the way from Italy, did a bit of landscaping, then ran for the hills when called upon to do the maintenance he'd promised (and been paid) to do.

Nothing left but to do it ourselves. I've planted a little yoke called a campanula (I think). I water it every day. I'm following its progress with interest. I can't believe this is happening to me . . .

First published in *Irish Tatler*, August 1999.

Driving Along in My Automobile

As if buying a house and starting to garden wasn't enough . . .

I'm learning to drive. I know it's no biggie, that I'm probably the only mid-thirties person in Ireland who can't yet drive, but I think I'm *it*. I've spent most of my life being a right scaredy-cat, having to cadge lifts off those normal people who'd felt the fear and done it anyway. So I finally decided to cop on to myself, and on a recent bank holiday I repaired to the Sandyford industrial estate with my husband and his Mazda.

We parked in a nice, quiet cul-de-sac, and I got into the driving seat. My first time behind the wheel I was literally trembling with terror. Then I looked into the rear-view mirror and it was like being in a parallel universe.

Himself explained the rudiments of driving and away we went. But the second I got the car moving forward I was appalled by the power of it and instantly slammed on the brakes. Then I reversed, and once again hit the brakes as soon as any movement was detected. Forwards we screeched again, then backwards. This continued for a very long time and when I finally finished I looked at Himself. He was doing his best to seem calm, but his clenched knuckles were the palest green. I decided I'd better get proper lessons.

I was warned that driving instructors could be a bit weird. Everyone had a story for me – that their instructor had been lecherous or racist or good, plain, old-fashioned bonkers. I thought they were only trying to cajole me to go ahead with the lessons, but to my great delight my instructor was awful! He was a sour-faced old boy who had no platitudes along the lines of 'Lep in behind the wheel there, sure we'll have you driving to Clare in no time, heh, heh, heh.' He didn't even introduce himself, just barked that he was taking me to a quiet road where I could do some driving without doing much damage. In an attempt to bond, I asked him how long he'd been a driving instructor. 'Too long,' he snapped, then we both lapsed into silence.

As we drove to the quiet road we passed a coloured gentleman, and me laddo beside me piped up, 'Sure, that fella would be more at home pulling coconuts out of a tree.'

I looked at him in astonishment. Was he having me on?

'I'm not racist,' he said defensively. 'I'm only saying.'

But minutes later, when we passed a crowd of young Asian people, your man chortled, 'Mind we don't drive into them. We'll be having Chinese takeaway for tea.'

It was then that I started looking around for the hidden camera.

Once parked on the quiet road, I was itching to actually do a bit of driving with the safety of dual controls. But nothing doing. Instead he sat me in the car (the passenger side), and for forty minutes he bored and baffled me with hand-drawn diagrams of a car's engine. There was much talk of something called a 'biting point' and the importance of finding it. Finally, with only fifteen minutes left of the lesson, I was allowed into the driving seat.

'I'm nervous,' I admitted.

'Sure, what do you want to be nervous for?' he spat.

Next thing I knew I was driving! Certainly I was wobbling all over the road, we were moving at two miles an hour and when I braked we nearly went through the windscreen, but I was delighted. Your man, however, went mental. He began shouting, literally shouting, about how awful I was. And it struck me that there was something awry here – if I'd wanted to be shouted at I'd have got one of my relations to teach me.

When I tried to remind Mr Instructor that it was my first time actually driving, he was having none of it. Off we went again, with me jerking and screeching up the road in stop-start fashion, as I acquainted myself with the accelerator. Once again he went bananas, shouting about how he wanted something called 'ladylike acceleration' from me.

'What if I was a man? Would you want ladylike acceleration from him?' I asked. I'm normally pathologically meek, but he was so unpleasant it was almost a joke. It was easy to stand up for myself.

The funniest thing of all was that at the end of the hour he expected me to sign up for a course of lessons with him. I told him to shag off. (Actually, I'm only showing off now. I mumbled something about having changed my mind, then fled.)

Then I got myself a woman instructor. A lovely, placid woman who barely winced when I came within an inch of taking the side off a row of parked cars, who hardly twitched when I slammed on the accelerator instead of the brakes. All the same, whenever she was late I used to pray that I'd got it wrong, that I didn't really have a lesson at all.

Since I've started driving my right hand has curled up into a type of claw. I grip the wheel so tightly that when I park and switch off the engine, it takes me ages to unpeel my hand. The mark of the steering wheel is now permanently embossed on my palm. And after a short time in the car, no matter how cold the day, the sweat is pouring off me.

And my language, colourful at the best of times, has gone to hell entirely. I live in terror of hurting anyone and any obstacles make me freak with panic: parked cars, moving cars, buses, suicidal pedestrians, horses and carriages, and worst of all, cyclists. In theory I approve of cyclists. I think they're cool because they're not adding to the pollution or traffic problems. But as I drive behind them all I can think of is how fragile and vulnerable they look. I'd never overtake them except for the mile-long row of cars crawling in my wake, beeping and threatening to kill me. So I gather up all my courage and veer out and overtake the cyclist. Then seconds later I've to stop at a traffic light and the bloody cyclist whizzes up on the inside, and as soon as the lights change I've to try and overtake them all over again.

But things have improved. At least people are now allowed to speak while I'm driving. In the early days even the sound of my passenger breathing was enough to put me off my stride. And the nightmares are fewer. At the start, I spent every night driving in my sleep and waking up, sitting bolt upright in the bed, my heart pounding because I'd had yet another dream of the car veering out of control.

A few months ago I bought a Nissan Micra and I'm besotted with it. I almost feel like a grown-up. Fishing around in my handbag, unable to find my car keys, is one of the most empowering experiences I've ever had!

First published in *Irish Tatler*, February 2000.

Reversing Around Corners

S ome time ago I wrote about how I was learning to drive. I wasn't very good but I was doing my best, so when Barbara, my driving instructor, suggested that I apply for a driving test, I decided I might as well. Anyway, the waiting lists were so long I'd somehow managed to convince myself that driving tests – like being abducted by aliens – only happened to other people.

Until one day a couple of months ago a manila envelope arrived for me. Unawares, I opened it, thinking it was probably just another narky letter from the tax office. But one glance at the page in front of me changed everything. I saw two words: 'Driving' and 'Test'. Suddenly I heard a roaring in my ears. The page fluttered from my fingers. Everything went black and I knew no more.

When I came to, I appeared to be in considerable distress and yelling about being 'picked on'. I had every intention of cancelling the test. Faking a broken leg or something. Then I faced facts – I was going to have to do it at some stage, it might as well be now. 'You won't pass it,' Tadhg confidently assured me. 'But it'll be good practice for you.'

Right.

I hadn't been a bad driver over the preceding few months. But from the moment I knew I'd be sitting my test four weeks hence, I turned into a quivering disaster. I stalled every five yards. I forgot to take the hand brake off. I turned on the windscreen wipers when I wanted to indicate.

And everyone I spoke to had a test horror story.

Julie, the girl who waxes my legs, told me about a friend of hers who'd knocked down and killed a dog during her test. 'Isn't that awful?' she said.

'Yes,' I agreed. 'Did she pass?' She didn't.

Someone else had done their three-point turn on a road where they were cutting down tree branches, and got half a tree tangled up in their undercarriage, which caused the car to cut out. They didn't pass either.

Goaded on by my fear of failure, I signed up for hundreds more driving lessons. I managed to get Barbara. I liked her and she seemed to like me. Just as well – we were going to be seeing an awful lot of one another.

Unfortunately, I'd managed to pick up loads of bad habits: cruising in neutral the last hundred yards or so to the traffic lights; never ever using my rear-view mirror because I was only interested in what I was driving towards and had no interest at all in what was behind me. And another side-effect of the forthcoming test was that I totally lost the ability to distinguish between left and right.

'Take the next left,' Barbara would say.

'Right you are,' I'd reply heartily, flicking on the windscreen wipers and moving into the right-hand lane.

I had lesson after lesson, and some days I thought I detected an improvement and other days it was clear I'd been hallucinating. It was the reversing around a corner that was nearly the death of me: I either mounted the kerb or ended up on the other side of the road with no idea of how I'd got there. More than once I pounded the steering wheel and cried with frustration at my own crapness.

Barbara was patient and encouraging, and one of the pieces of advice she gave me was to check that I'd got the date and time correct for my test. Which I did a couple of days before the big day. I was on the phone at the time and fiddling with stuff, you know the way you do. Multi-tasking. I can talk *and* rub funny stains on the table at the same time. Holding my own in a conversation about (as I seem to remember) the merits of Matthew McConaughey over Ben Affleck, I eased my test notification out from under a pile of bills. And my heart nearly stopped.

I had the date right. I even had the time right. But the location was wrong. Somehow, in all the fuss when the notification had arrived, I'd come to the conclusion that I was being tested in Churchtown – which was why I'd spent every waking moment of the previous three weeks driving the highways and byways of Churchtown. So much so that if I missed a day people began to worry that they hadn't seen me. However, I'd got it wrong. I wasn't sitting my driving test in Churchtown, I was sitting it in Rathgar. Rathgar – of which I knew nothing. Not one tricky roundabout, not one unexpected sliproad, not one difficult right turn.

The letters danced before my eyes, then stood still just long enough for me to realize the full extent of the horror, then off they started skipping again with nah-nah-nah-naaah-nah glee. Somehow, stutteringly, I managed to sustain the conversation while the sweat poured off me in buckets. Eventually I slammed the phone down, turned to Himself and screeched, 'Come on!'

'Come on where? It's half ten at night.'

'Come on, we're going to Rathgar to practise the test route!'

The day before the test I had a dress rehearsal – which was a disaster. My hill start was a non-starter and my three-point turn ended up being a twenty-three-point one with me ricocheting off each kerb like a tennis ball. Both Barbara and I were very subdued. Barbara had the decency to pretend that she had a leak in her bathroom on her mind, but I knew it was my fault. Who could blame her for being disappointed – all those lessons and would you look at the state of me?

Then the dreaded day dawned and Himself came with me to provide moral support. I'd barely slept – really, I mean it, it was six in the morning before I'd nodded off, and I was up again at eight. I was certain that I was going to fail, never more certain of anything in my life.

The test centre was what I imagine Hell's waiting-room is like. Everyone was grey-pale and dumb with terror. And then my name was called . . .

I'd been led to believe that driving testers were barely human. That they were forty-five-year-old men who still lived at home with their mammies, that they wore anoraks teamed with suit trousers which exhibited a permanent crease and that they carried clipboards even on their days off. But to my great surprise, I got a girl. And she was nice. Well, not nice *nice*, like someone trying to sell you lip-gloss, but not a desocialized weirdo either.

We sat in a little cubicle and she asked me questions – who can drive on a motorway, when can you overtake on the left, what my favourite colour is (actually, maybe I imagined that bit). It all went OK, but that wasn't the part of the test I was worried about. And the next thing, feeling like I was dreaming, I was walking towards my car with her.

When we were both sitting in the car I tried licking up to her by asking if she'd like the heating on, but she just said nicely but firmly, 'Don't worry about me. Just drive the way you'd normally drive.' I resisted the urge to throw my head back and cackle hysterically. And then we were off.

The whole thing was like an out-of-body experience. My heart was pounding, my mouth was as dry as carpet, my head was light and I could feel the blood pulsing through me. Left turns and right turns and traffic lights and roundabouts all happened in a faraway haze. The hill start seemed to go all right. The reversing around the corner wasn't one of my best, but I didn't mount the kerb or somehow end up mysteriously on the other side of the road. My three-point turn ended up being five points, but with an absence of kerb bumpage. As we finally headed back to the test centre I wasn't aware of having done anything heinously wrong, but you never know. One person had told me they were failed for taking their left hand off the steering wheel to scratch their leg. Another for having her hands in a quarter-to-four position instead of ten-to-two.

After I'd parked, she announced that we would go back inside to get the results. I couldn't understand why she couldn't tell me in the car, but apparently it's because there's a danger that they might be attacked by a disappointed candidate. I trooped inside after her, and when we sat down in her little cubicle she declared, 'You have passed the test.' Immediately I burst into tears and she wasn't a bit fazed. It obviously happens all the time.

I waited to suddenly feel grown-up – everyone had promised me that I would. But nothing happened. Looks like I'm going to spend the rest of my life convinced I'm still sixteen and waiting for my exam results.

I skipped back out to the waiting-room, where the next batch of people waiting to do their tests were sitting like the souls of the damned. Mindful of their nerves I grabbed Himself, waved my bit of paper and hissed triumphantly, 'I passed, I passed, I passed, I passed!'

Two days later I drove my car into the gatepost.

First published in *Irish Tatler*, July 2000.

The Pissed is a Foreign Country, They Do Things Differently There

No one sets out to be an alcoholic. It certainly wasn't part of my life plan, but it happened anyway. Luckily I was one of the fortunate ones. At the start of 1994 I got help and was able to stop, which was when the real business of growing up began.

I was nine years old, standing in the kitchen, when suddenly I was assailed by a fierce urge for *something*. My body literally spasmed with it. It was far more than a desperate emotional yearning; this was a panicky physical need. Thirst to the power of a million. My head raced through my usual panaceas – fizzy drinks, chocolate – but none of them would have quenched this raging desire. The same raging desire that was my constant companion twenty years later. I was a precocious child who knew about alcoholism, and a little voice inside me went 'Oh oh.'

There was nothing in my upbringing to indicate that by the time I was thirty I'd be drinking on my own, mired in denial, living in the wreckage of a ruined life. I came from an ordinary family and had loving parents, who were moderate drinkers. There was no childhood trauma or disaster that I could hang the blame on.

But from an early age there was something definitely adrift with me – feelings of crippling self-consciousness and self-loathing. I felt as though I'd been born without life's rule book. I was so out of step with the world around me, I sometimes wondered if I was from another planet.

Feelings of impending doom tormented me. I became convinced that our house would burn down during the night, so I took to filling up basins of water in the bathroom every evening, for speedier fire-fighting when the time came. I went through a phase of wearing my nightdress over my uniform because I was so terrified of being late for school.

So when I had my first drink in my teens, I thought I'd found the secret of the universe. The fear disappeared and all at once I felt as good as everyone else. There and then I decided that I would never again do anything difficult or painful without this wonderful substance, alcohol. Why turn my back on help?

That first drink was vodka and one of the other girls refused to drink it because it tasted disgusting. Never mind the taste, I thought, baffled. Feel the *effect*.

Even though I didn't drink very often in my teens, once I started drinking, I could never get enough. Right from the very beginning I drank more and faster than everyone else. And right from the very beginning I woke up with killer shame and dread. Guilt at what I'd done the night before. It was never anything too risqué – usually something to do with snogging boys that I shouldn't have – but it was sufficiently out of character for me to be mortified.

When I was eighteen I went to college to study law — I'd always been academically bright and hopes were high (although not mine). I got a fairly decent degree and it was expected that I'd become a solicitor. But I couldn't do it. I was paralysed by *something*, which I couldn't articulate. So I left Dublin and went to London and got a job as a waitress. It was a glaring example of self-sabotage. Only now can I see that it was my old trouble, acute self-hatred, that wouldn't let me have a decent job. I simply felt that I didn't deserve it.

Eventually, I got a job in an accounts office. Once I had more money, my drinking moved up several notches. Albeit excessive, it remained social for a long time. I didn't yet drink on my own — that was all still ahead of me in my empty future. And everyone else seemed to drink as much as I did — it hadn't occurred to me that I tried hard to surround myself with other heavy drinkers so that my drinking didn't stand out.

Fun became my yardstick. It was important to have 'fun' while drunk and more 'fun' when doing morning-after post-mortems. ('It must have been a brilliant night. I don't remember a thing.') I distanced myself from my drunken behaviour by turning it into entertaining anecdotes. One morning I woke up to find a carton of french fries scattered under my pillow with no idea of how they'd got there. But I sidestepped my shock by working it up into a funny story. My drinking wasn't a problem, I told myself, it was *fun*.

I was big on bravado. I could drink neat whiskey without a shudder. I could down an entire pint in one go. I could and did drink anything and I rarely threw up. I could outdrink men twice my size and I thought this was *sexy*.

I was a woman in her twenties, living in London. Wasn't it about wild times, raucous high spirits, ending up at strange parties, about embracing spontaneity? And if I sometimes woke up in an unfamiliar flat with people I didn't know, surely it was better than being boring?

OK, so I was perpetually in debt, I woke up covered in bruises with no memory of how I'd got them, I often missed work because I was hungover, the depressions following a good night out were getting worse, I seemed to do nothing *but* drink, I never saw the second half of a play, I got off with men who turned my stomach when I sobered up and relationships with men I liked never worked out. At least I was *living*. It was a constant search for drama, any kind of activity, so that I – had I but known it – didn't have to be alone with myself. And if some things had to be jettisoned along the way, like self-respect, then so what?

But alcoholism is a subtle, insidious and progressive disease. Which meant, quite simply, that I got worse.

I can't say exactly at what point I became physiologically as well as psychologically addicted. But definitely by my late twenties, through overexposure, my body was sensitized to alcohol. So that when I drank anything – no matter how small – it triggered a fierce craving for more and more. Once I started I literally could not stop. And once I stopped I couldn't stay stopped. I had become – though I wouldn't have known the term – a binge drinker.

But there were enough pockets of normality to paper over the problem – I went shopping, bought shoes I didn't need and couldn't afford, went to the gym, met friends for dinner, had nights in with my flatmates watching soaps, and apart from being increasingly unreliable, I was actually good at my job.

And yet . . .

I kind of strayed into drinking in the mornings. It started at weekends, where a combination of the terrible depression of a hangover and the unbearability of having a lonely, empty day stretching ahead of me meant I couldn't stop myself from picking up the bottle. But over the months, the weekend drinking spilled over into Monday and Tuesday. Or began on Thursday. Or Wednesday.

Even as I write this, my head tightens with disbelief. But at the time my denial blocked out all light. I didn't know that denial is as big a part of alcoholism as the drinking, that it grows in direct proportion to it, so that I was constantly normalizing the abnormal. Bizarre as it sounds, I didn't think I was an alcoholic. I knew something was very wrong, but I didn't – *couldn't* – make the connection between my acute misery and my drinking. Because then I might have had to do something about it – like give up. And that was out of the question.

Around me my friends, my peers, had begun to do peculiar things – like get married, buy flats, have children, get promoted. As my drinking buddies fell by the wayside, I was frightened. Their achievements highlighted the emptiness, the lack of forward propulsion in my own life. So I chose to mock them. 'So and so has become the most boring person alive,' I regularly scorned. 'All he wants to talk about is his new couch and his career path.'

I didn't have a career. As it was, it was only because I had a concerned and sympathetic boss that I held on to my job. And I most certainly didn't have a healthy relationship with a man. By my late twenties, I had developed an uncanny ability to find men who could endorse my self-loathing.

But when things that happen to alcoholics began happening to me, I was appalled. One night, after I'd been on a solitary three-day binge, I went for a drink with my – for want of a better word – boyfriend. To my horror, I found that my hands had such tremors I literally couldn't pick up my glass. Although it was obvious to everyone who knew me that this was likely to happen, I was still devastated and disbelieving. Even now I can see the expression on his face – realization and contempt.

The night I first made the decision to stay in and get drunk on my own, that I'd rather have alcohol than people, was when I began the descent into the final phase of my alcoholism. It was St Patrick's night 1993, and just before I left to join my friends in the revelling, it struck me how much more convenient it would be to stay home. I could drink as much as I liked without anyone looking askance at me. What could be simpler?

It was around then that I stopped eating. I'd always been fond of food, overeating as a form of comfort and then overexercising as a form of penance. But as though a switch had flipped, I just stopped. Lots of the time I was too sick to eat, but mostly I'd just lost interest in food. My love for alcohol was so passionate there was no room for anything else.

By then it was glaringly obvious to everyone around me that I had a serious problem. Concerned friends and colleagues began to bandy the word 'alcoholic' about. To get them off my back, I pretended I agreed with them. I promised I'd stop drinking. But I was looking from the inside out, where the view was very different – a life without alcohol was unliveable. Anyway, alcoholism only happened to other people. But even though I couldn't possibly be an alcoholic, I was unable to stop drinking. Sometimes I managed a few days, but sooner or later I always cracked.

My life dwindled away to almost nothing, until all I was left with was a defensive position. I spent bright sunny days hiding in darkened rooms. I missed more and more work, got further and further into debt, lost friend after friend. And I didn't care. So long as I had my best friend, my lover, alcohol, I didn't need anyone or anything else.

From September 1993 to January 1994 was the most bereft time I have ever lived through. I had a bare bed, in a bare room, with a bare window, in a bare, bare life. The cold seeped through the naked glass and I isolated myself as completely as I could, not seeing anyone, not answering the phone. I was paranoid and fearful and only went out to buy more alcohol.

I read a lot of Charles Bukowski and Raymond Carver

around then, taking comfort especially from Bukowski's stoic acceptance that while alcohol made him sick and crazy, it was possible, indeed *necessary*, to co-exist with it. And three lines from a Raymond Carver poem jumped out at me, when he's describing perfect happiness – 'No one home, no one coming home, and all I can drink.' That's me, I thought. I felt understood by a kindred spirit and I read those three lines over and over, like a mantra. I'd always been prone to depression and melancholy, but it got worse. I began to have suicidal fantasies. When I closed my eyes, I was overwhelmed by a picture of me blowing my head off with a gun. At times in a busy street it was almost more than I could bear not to sink to my knees and *howl* with the agony of being alive. Before I went to sleep at night I used to pray not to wake up. For every moment that I wasn't unconscious I felt as though my head was a war zone.

Things accelerated until, in hellish misery, one Monday morning I jerked into consciousness. I'd had my, by now, usual weekend, alone and drunk. I was in the horrors, savagely depressed, and something ripped inside me. Suddenly I couldn't live my unbearable life any longer and for the first time I made the connection that alcohol was responsible for my wretched state. But I'd tried so many times to stop drinking and I hadn't been able to. I was trapped in a pit, and suicide seemed my only option. Hardly believing what I was doing, I swallowed every pill I could find and waited to die. But as I drifted into unconsciousness, I had a moment of clarity. Maybe I had another option, maybe I *could* live without alcohol.

I rang a friend, who rang an ambulance. I spent six weeks in rehab before re-emerging into the world.

It was like the end of a love affair, the most passionate of my life. The gig was up, I knew I couldn't handle alcohol but I raged against the loss. I was thirty. I felt like my life was over and I braced myself to endure the next forty or so years. Without drink, I felt I'd never be happy again – which is funny because I hadn't been happy with it.

They'd told me in rehab to stick close to other recovering alcoholics, which I did, but reluctantly. By now I was half-prepared to admit that I was an alcoholic, but I still felt special and different – not realizing that, amongst other things, alcoholism is a disease of terminal uniqueness.

I had my last drink in January, but suddenly it was August, something good blossomed within me and I remember miracles.

I remember it was summer, that it stayed summer for a very long time.

I remember the absence of fear.

I remember the conviction that nothing bad could happen to me.

I remember feeling young and ripe with hope.

I remember being as excited as if I'd just moved to London, though I'd lived there for eight years.

I remember how sharp and new life was, how the old one seemed shrouded in grey mist.

I remember buying curtains for my bedroom window –

glorious blues and greens, instead of the colour of air, the no-colour of my old life.

I remember walking through the crowds of Portobello Road one Saturday afternoon and the feeling of invisibility that true belonging brings.

I remember the thrill of rediscovery.

I remember feeling in love with everyone.

I remember the pit-of-my-stomach happiness at being me, at being clean and sober and honest.

I remember lying on sundrenched grass in Soho Square, laughing at something someone had said, and being struck by the understanding that even though I'd been so very careless of myself and my safety through the drinking years, nothing terrible had ever befallen me – and I remember the strangest thing of all. For someone who'd always felt so inconsequential I remember realizing that I'd been rescued. That I'd been worth rescuing.

Previously unpublished.

TWELVE MONTHS

Sackcloth, Ashes . . . and the Gym

January. The sackcloth and ashes month. The hairshirt and self-flagellation month. The month when I repent for my sins, when I do penance for the hedonistic free-for-all that was Christmas.

January, the month when bitter, bleak winds sweep across the empty plains of my bank account.

January, the month when I open my credit-card statement and my mouth drops open in outrage. Someone must have stolen my card and gone berserk buying gift packs in the Body Shop, I conclude. Just as I pick up the phone to call the police, I realize the person was me.

For me, January is always a month of sensory deprivation – no going out, no buying anything – as a direct result of the crazed orgy of spending on so many useless things during the frantic countdown to the big day. Never in the field of human consumption was so much spent by so many on such a multitude of little raffia baskets filled with bathsalts, facecloths and white musk body-lotion. While the credit cards are having a rest I have to make my own entertainment, so I while away the first thirty-one days of the year on my knees, picking pine needles out of the carpet. I have wheedly conversations with myself where I try to summon the energy to put the Christmas tree out with the rubbish. On the rare years that I achieve this, I'm a nervous wreck, tensed against being woken early on bin day by the binmen roaring insults up at my bedroom window when they discover the seven-foot tree nestling un-inconspicuously amongst the black bags.

Luckily, though, the tree usually ends up staying until June. Then when someone volunteers to carry it outside, I say, 'Ah no. It's nearly Christmas again. It might as well stay. It'll save us buying a new one.'

But most of all, January is the month of regrets, and now it's pay-back time. Time to undo the damage during the January purge, with self-denial and fresh starts. Except I'm not going to. This year the only thing I'm giving up is giving up. I couldn't be bothered anymore. I've been on a diet for most of my adult life and I'm fatter now than I've ever been.

I am living proof that dieting makes you fat. But don't for a minute think that I'm going to come back to you in a couple of months' time and say that since I gave up dieting I've lost weight. Because I was conned by that particular trick a couple of years back. 'Take the mystique out of food,' they said. 'Eat what you like,' they urged. 'Reclaim your right to eat and you'll break the starve-and-binge cycle.' 'Right, thanks very much, I will,' I said, suspicious, yet delighted. Well, it didn't work. I put on *more* weight and the one person who wasn't surprised was me.

The only times in my life that I've ever been skinny were when I was having a couple of what amounted to near nervous breakdowns. And even when I was at my thinnest, there was always a fat woman inside me waiting to get out. So now, if I was offered the choice between being plump and happy or skinny and miserable, I'm nearly certain I'd choose the plump and happy option. Truly, I have achieved wisdom! (All the same, I wouldn't object if I was offered the chance to do a bit of barter – a 10 per cent reduction in my peace of mind in exchange for a corresponding reduction in the size of my thighs, for example.)

To banish the superfluous lard acquired over the festive season, January is the month when gyms around the world see a surge in membership. When poor awkward people emerge from changing rooms, resplendent in their pristine new leotards and snow-white runners that you could sail to France on, hugging the wall, convinced that everyone is looking at them and laughing. Which indeed they are. My experience is that most people feel so anxious in gyms that if someone else is at even more of a disadvantage than they are, they will cruelly capitalize on it. All the better to convince themselves that *they're* OK.

This January I won't be joining a gym. But only because I'm already a member. In the same way that I've been on a diet almost since the day my mother put me on to solids, I've belonged to a gym since nearly the first day I began walking. It's not my fault. I lived in London during the soulless greedy eighties when you were no one if you didn't own an Azzedine Alaia dress, have a cappuccino machine and belong to a gym. And it wasn't enough just to belong to a gym – you had to go at bizarre times. Either you got up at four-thirty and did two hours' circuit training before going to your flash job in media or the City, or else you went after you finished work at midnight. No other times would do. (Which was hard for me because I worked the shamefully slothful hours of ten to six.)

The worst thing about joining a gym – no matter what month of the year – is The Fitness Assessment, where they tell you how fat and unfit you are before they let you loose on the machines. I had a very humiliating one about three years back, after I'd taken a six-month sabbatical from step classes. First they weighed me (I always close my eyes, because it's invariably worse than I expect it to be). Then they measured my percentage body fat with a kind of pliers' yoke (again, I requested to be spared the details). Next I had to lep up on a bike and cycle for five minutes at top speed to assess my aerobic fitness. Then I had to pull and lift things so that they could find out how strong I was. Then all the information was fed into a computer and within seconds a print-out appeared which gave a picture of my overall fitness.

The assessor's face went very still. 'One moment,' she said through white lips. 'I just want to get my superior.'

The superior arrived and they both studied the print-out. Low muttered conversation ensued. 'That can't be right . . .' drifted over to me, as I sat with a fixed, anxious smile on my face. It seemed they thought the computer was broken. So they did the whole thing again, and it turned out that the computer wasn't broken. Although I could have told them that.

The superior went to get his superior. In fact they almost rang staff on their day off to come in and have a gawk at me.

Judging by the things they were saying – 'An unexpectedly high percentage of fat . . . In all my years . . . Very poor muscle tone . . .' – they'd never seen the like.

'You don't *look* that bad,' the assessor said, by way of comfort.

My humiliation was utter. Nowadays, I ask to be excused from The Fitness Assessment. I say, 'Lookit, I'll pay the twenty quid anyway. But you know and I know that I'm unfit and overweight. Can't we just leave it at that?'

So there we are! Sorry for all the doom and gloom, but that's January for you. And let's not forget that spring is just around the corner.

Happy New Year!

First published in *Irish Tatler*, January 1998.

Have You the Green Food Colouring?

S tanding in the perishing cold, half a lawn hanging out of
the lapel of my good coat, unable to see over people's
heads as yet another pipe band marches past – what else could
it be but Saint Patrick's Day!

During my childhood during the dim and distant sixties
and seventies, when we had to make our own entertainment,
Saint Patrick's Day was almost as good as Christmas. OK, so
we didn't get presents, but we got little gold harps to stick on
our collars. And fair enough, no one liked having to go to
Mass and sing 'Hail glorious Saint Patrick, dear saint of our
isle,' but on the good side we got the day off school. And
even though the parade never really *delivered* – not enough
Disney characters, none in fact, and there was always just that
one brass band too many – I still got excited.

Of course, it's different now. During the eleven years that
I lived abroad, the Patrick's Day parade in Dublin under-
went a fundamental metamorphosis and became a reconsti-
tuted, rehabilitated, international extravaganza. Instead of
the interminable ranks of khaki-clad army brass bands,
there are now crews of dusky young girls from the
Notting Hill carnival, shivering past in spangly bikinis

and elaborate head-dresses, doing a lack-lustre wine' in the inclement March elements. (Unfortunately, they couldn't upgrade the weather in the same way they did the rest of the parade.)

And instead of the one crappy float with a banner saying something like 'Buy Our Bread' (let's just say) and some poor mortified eejit dressed as a loaf of bread, half-heartedly waving to the masses below, there are now elaborate mini-worlds passing by on each lorry. Music and good-looking men and jugglers and fire-eaters and ... oh ... all *kinds* of things. Although to be honest, the thing that got the biggest cheer at the parade last year was when a French fire-juggler dropped one of his torches on his leg and the bottom of his trousers went up in flames. The frenzied dance that he did to put himself out was greeted with raucous laughter from the crowds of spectators lining the road, who then attempted to mimic him. But even though Saint Patrick's Day is the annual twenty-four hours when we celebrate our Irishness, ironically enough, the most memorable and enjoyable ones I've ever had were when I was living and working in *England*.

There were two other Irish people working in the same office as me, and every year we tried and every year we failed to convince our boss that we should be allowed to have the seventeenth of March off – in order to go to an Irish pub in Kilburn or Cricklewood that we'd never usually go near, eat free bacon and cabbage, smoke twenty Major, get mouldy drunk, give out about England, sing maudlin songs about how we wished we were back home in the Emerald Isle, and generally savour our Hibernianness.

'It's our right as Irish people,' we complained bitterly. 'Jewish people get Jewish holidays off. We're being discriminated against.'

Then my boss gently explained that if any Jewish employees were missing in action on Jewish holidays, it simply meant that they were using up their annual leave. 'You're perfectly welcome to take a day of your holidays,' she said. Which we declined, while we muttered darkly amongst ourselves about invoking the ancient Irish tradition of throwing a sickie.

But the self-same boss who wouldn't give us a free day off made every other effort to make the occasion special. She had been brought up in Columbus's Circle in New York, which was full of Irish people, so she knew the drill. Without fail, on a Patrick's Day morning she'd arrive in with enough clumps of shamrock, green rosettes or little tricolour ribbons for everyone. We never knew how she'd got her hands on them – such articles were like gold dust in central London. We could only presume that as she lived near the Archway, she was well in with someone who was able to see her right. 'Ask no questions,' she'd say, tapping her nose.

But we did, anyway. 'Have you the soda bread?' we'd demand, looking at the parcels under her arm. 'Did you bring the decorations? I hope you didn't forget the cassette player? Have you the tape of the Kilfenora Ceili Band? Did you remember the red lemonade? Were you able to get the carton of Tayto? Have you the green food colouring?'

The badges would be distributed amongst the staff, who were a bit of a multinational crew – Irish, American, St Lucian, Australian. Even one or two English people often ended up sporting a tricolour ribbon with a gold paper harp glued to it. (We enjoyed that, so we did.)

Then we set about turning the office into a little corner of Ireland. Green, orange and white streamers festooned the walls and computers; Irish reels and jigs played all day – or at least until someone decided they couldn't bear any more and hid the tape; visiting colleagues had red lemonade or green mineral water pressed upon them; or were invited to have a slice of soda bread or a packet of Tayto. Then when they'd eaten it, with traditional Irish hospitality we'd insist that they have another, that there wasn't a pick on them, that they were fading away before our very eyes. And then we'd try to force one more on them.

The atmosphere was absolutely fantastic. Anyone who came in left in great humour. No mean feat, as we were an accounts office, whose duty it was to ruin people's lives by telling them that we'd lost their expenses claim or put them on an inhumanely punitive tax code, or whatever.

And when the whistle blew at six o'clock, the cans and bottles were hauled out from under the desks, where they'd been biding their time since early morning. And so, some hours later than strictly preferable, we all proceeded to get mouldy drunk, smoke twenty Major, give out about England

and sing maudlin songs until the porter begged us to leave.
All together now! 'Hail glorious Saint Patrick, dear saint of
our isle . . .'

First published in *Irish Tatler*, March 1999.

Thanks, Mam

Mothers' Day wasn't invented when I was small. Or if it was, I didn't know about it. But suddenly in my early teens it seemed to appear out of nowhere, and everyone blamed the Americans. 'A load of cod,' one of my more curmudgeonly schoolteachers pronounced. (He was a man.) 'The bloody Yanks with their *Starsky and Hutch*, and their pagan feasts. There'll be Uncle's Day and Third-Cousin-Twice-Removed's Day and Pet Rabbit's Day soon if we're not careful.'

He urged us to boycott Mothers' Day, to take a stand against cultural imperialism. And because I wanted to preserve my pocket-money for the truly important things in life, like fizzy cola-bottles and Creme Eggs, I was happy to go along with him.

Except peer pressure was too great. Oneupmanship among teenage girls is vicious and I was interrogated repeatedly. 'What are you getting your mum for Mothers' Day?' Reluctantly I realized I'd better get with the program.

But I just wasn't into it. I was selfish, self-obsessed and astonishingly ungrateful for everything my mother had done for me. After all, I was a *teenager*, it was part of my job description. So on the appointed Sunday morning, when I appeared at my mother's bedside and said, 'For feeding me, clothing me, minding me, worrying about me since the day I was born, for the eighteen hours you spent in labour with me, when epidurals were still only a twinkle in a scientist's eye, here's a £2.99 bunch of daffodils,' I felt that she was getting the better part of the bargain. That I was the one who'd been ripped off.

Over the next couple of years, Mothers' Day quickly became part of the landscape. Except my brothers, sisters and I were never prepared. In the week before it, there was always a queue of us sidling up to our mother.

'Mam,' we'd wheedle. 'Can I have some money?'

'What for?' she'd ask suspiciously. 'Money doesn't grow on trees/I'm not made of money/Who do you think I am – that fella Onassis?' (Tick as preferred.)

'It's for you,' we'd say huffily. 'For Mothers' Day. To buy you a present.'

'No. I've advanced you your pocket money until next September. Enough is enough.'

'Janey! Talk about ungrateful.'

And then, of course, there were the Mothers' Day lunches. Which, naturally, for a celebration of family gratitude and unity, caused a huge number of passionate rows. The big problem about Mothering Sunday was that it very inconveniently fell on a *Sunday*. Which didn't suit at all in my late teens, when it was my habit to go out on a Saturday night, get jarred, stay the night in a friend's house and only be able to get the bus home when the nausea had subsided, some time on Sunday evening. In the days running up to the lunch, my poor father, with a mixture of threats and pleas, was like a sheepdog trying to round up my four siblings and me. And in fairness, we did usually turn up. But, gracious to the last, someone always said, thirty seconds before we went out the door to the restaurant, 'Mam, will you iron me something to wear for this Mothers' Day lunch yoke Dad is making us go to?'

But worse than being ungracious about Mothers' Day is when you totally forget about it. You'd wonder how anyone could, when there are so many reminders of it, but people do. One Wednesday last year, when the restaurant I'd booked to take my mammy to on the big day rang to say they were full after all, Himself took the call. As I watched him talking, I wondered why he'd gone so pale. The minute he slammed down the phone he announced he was going out.

'Where to?' I asked.

'Card shop,' he gasped. 'How many days does it take to get a card to England?'

At least he'd remembered on a Wednesday. Woe betide the poor misfortunate who doesn't remember until Saturday evening, when it's far, far too late. Normally you can hardly get up Grafton Street on a Saturday, what with flower-stalls waylaying you and dogging your path. But on the eve of Mothering Sunday, not a single flower is left in the whole of the Western World. Flower shops turn into a wasteland. An overturned bucket or perhaps a scrap of cellophane is all that remains after the hordes have been through.

And don't think you'll get away with buying chocolates instead. Oh no! I know several people who, with a flourish, presented a box of Roses, only to be told, tight-lipped, 'I've given up chocolate for Lent,' Mothers' Day usually being awkward enough to fall during the Catholic version of Ramadan.

But I'm no longer a selfish teenager. I'm in my thirties now and my mother is my friend. So I'd just like to take the opportunity this Mothers' Day to say, 'Mammy, for feeding me, clothing me, minding me, worrying about me since the day I was born, for the eighteen hours you spent in labour with me, when epidurals were still only a twinkle in a scientist's eye – thank you.'

First published in the *Sunday Independent*, March 1998.

Time's Arrow

*G*etting old – it's a dirty job, but someone's got to do it. And the honour, this month, has fallen to me. It's my birthday, d'you see? And actually, considering my great age, I don't feel too bad. Birthdays (mine anyway) have traditionally been a time of great weeping, gnashing of teeth (the few I have left) and pulling out of hair (ditto). When I take stock and find myself very, very wanting. Like New Year's Eve, though probably not as bad.

Past birthday celebrations have been rather mournful affairs. 'Happy birthday!' friends and family exclaim rather hysterically, in an attempt to cancel out my incessant intoning of 'I am a fat, useless failure.'

'Did you get nice pres—'

'I am a fat, useless failure.'

'That's a lovely card. Who's it fr—'

'I am a fat, useless failure.'

'Well, not exactly fat. Just very pear-shaped.'

'Fat. Don't patronize me, not on my birthday. I am a fat, useless fail . . .'

But in the last few years, for some unfathomable reason, birthdays haven't triggered my usual suicidal despair. It seems

I might be feeling my way to becoming – God forbid – *content*. There was a time when I thought that contentment was one of the worst things that could happen to me. Acute, confused unhappiness seemed far preferable. Edgy angst was the province of the young, as opposed to calm serenity, which smacked of plump, aged complacency and the desire to garden. (Let me stress that I'm not *very* calm or serene, but all these things are relative.)

It sneaks up on you, this ageing process. Once I knew and loved every song in the Top Twenty, but now I'm lucky to know even one, and I'm bound to think it's shite. (I mean, that S Club 7 – crap or what?) I don't know when this change happened. I've been going around, foolishly assuming that my finger is still on the pulse, but with each second that passes I'm inexorably slipping away from the centre of all that is fashionable and youthful. Becoming more and more marginalized and on the edges. There's nothing I can do about it. And the worst thing of all – I don't really care.

To show you how bad I am, I will readily admit:

a) My ears are the only parts of my body that are pierced.
b) The last time I was up at five in the morning was after seven hours of sleep.
c) I know very little about the Chemical Brothers.
d) I have only ever said 'Having it large' as a joke.

But this contentment wasn't easily won because being a thirty-something is like experiencing adolescence in reverse. Your body starts behaving in all these strange and outlandish ways and you're powerless to prevent it. Like, out of nowhere, your body starts wanting to stay in sometimes on a weekend night – and it's horrifying. Nearly as bad as when I started to grow hair under my arms. Not caning it on a Saturday evening seemed like terrible, shameful, aberrant behaviour. So if I succumbed and stayed in, I made millions of not-very-convincing excuses – long week, late night the night before, early start on Sunday, no clean clothes, pain in stomach, yadda yadda. But, even as I barricaded myself in with a video and a carton of Ben & Jerry's, I couldn't really enjoy myself. Convinced that everyone else in the whole universe was doing tequila slammers with dangerous men in ear-bleedingly loud nightclubs until five in the morning. That I was the only oul'-wan-before-her-time.

But this getting-old lark happens to nearly everyone. Even men! Though maybe they're less likely to notice immediately. There they are, blithely going around thinking they're still a bit of a young hep cat, until a person who is legitimately young decides to disabuse them of the idea. I was over at a friend's house, and her younger brother and a few of his mates were in the kitchen, smoking dope. Himself went into the kitchen (to make Ovaltine, probably), and when he saw the drug-ingesting that was going on there, got all excited. This is a man who, in his heyday, could roll joints with one hand. He doesn't get much opportunity any more, because . . . well, I don't know why. Because we're in our mid-thirties, I suppose. Anyway, there he was hanging around in the kitchen, waiting to be offered a toke, smiling and nodding at the youths, *thinking he was the same as them*, God love him. When the next moment one of the boys flung himself bodily across the kitchen to cover a lump of hash that was sitting, exposed, on the table. 'You should have seen their faces,' Himself lamented in shock. 'Like they thought I was an adult, or something. Like I was going to tell on them.'

He sat with his (grey) head in his (liver-spotted) hands for the best part of a week. 'I'm young,' he kept saying. 'I'm young.'

Now that I'm past my prime, I've had to let go of several visions or versions of myself. Better versions, of course. I used to think that being alive was some sort of apprenticeship where I'd get to a certain age and all of a sudden I'd be able to *do* life. That out of nowhere I'd know how to twirl my hair into a fabulous smooth French pleat. Or that the day would dawn when I'd just somehow be able to time my leg-waxes to coincide with good weather. Or that I'd wake up one morning and suddenly be one of those people who can go out in their slip and look willowy and graceful and fey and *right*. But now I accept that it's never going to happen, that I'd just look like I'd gone out without getting dressed.

As for the gym – I always felt that I wasn't working to my full potential, that if I could only go a couple more times a week I'd be looking like Kate Moss in no time. And that I'd get round to it as soon as the current busy/lazy/self-destructive phase passed. But now that will never be – it's too late for the gym to give me the perfect body. All it can do is stem the Jabba the Hutt tide.

But it's fine. The only weird thing is that, paradoxically, I still feel like a teenager. I'm still waiting to feel grown-up (as opposed to just getting old). I don't know how they do it, but everyone else seems to have it sussed. Even though I have many of the trappings of adulthood – George Michael CDs, a copy of *Allen Carr's Easy Way to Stop Smoking*, a monthly standing order to a pension fund, a good relationship with my neighbours, plump upper arms – I'm still waiting for that glorious moment when I truly *feel* like a grown-up. I suspect I'll probably proceed directly from adolesence to the menopause. Anyway, wheel out the birthday cake, I feel a Jabba the Hutt moment coming on . . .

First published in *Irish Tatler*, October 1999.

Feeling Sheepish

One of the hardest things about working from home is not having a Christmas party. All I have now to sustain me are memories . . . Before I gave up the day job in the accounts department, we used to have great Christmas parties. Tears, confessions, people getting sick or insulting their boss, no one in the next morning – oh, the glory days! But one year when funds were low, we had a choice between having no party at all or making all the food ourselves. For some reason, we opted for the latter.

It seemed like a good idea because we had a multi-racial staff. Ahmed, a Moroccan, offered to roast a couple of sheep on a spit in the courtyard. Apparently he had 'contacts' and could get his hands on a pair of dead sheep, no questions asked. The rest of the duties were shared out among the fifty administrative staff (the hundred academic staff were let off doing anything because they were regarded as too dippy to be depended on). People were variously responsible for bread, cheese, fruit, desserts, salads, starters and wine. The Irish members of staff (all three of us) were, naturally, put on baked-potato duty. We also seemed to be the natural inheritors of the mantle of coleslaw making, because of the cabbage element.

On the day of the party, the sons of Erin hung our black, crushed-velvet frocks on the back of the office door, rolled up our sleeves and repaired to a disused studio to make a literal mountain of coleslaw. All around the building others were making vats of trifle, slicing miles of bread, washing fields of lettuce, mixing gallons of thousand-island dressing. But, even while we catered like the clappers, things had to be kept ticking over in the offices too. I kept having to desist from chopping cabbages to attend to petty-cash duties. The best was when someone rushed in and gasped, 'Ahmed has arrived with the sheep. He needs money to pay for the taxi.'

Even though the sheep were long dead, I couldn't banish a mental image of Ahmed in a black London cab, squashed up beside two fat, fluffy sheep, like busty, old women buttoned up against the cold. As I went back to the office to get money, I half-expected to find the two sheep running amok through the hallowed corridors, as if they were cavorting along boreens in County Clare.

Next, the other paddies and I had to go to the nearby Tesco to buy up their entire stock of spuds. You need a lot of spuds to go around a hundred and fifty people. An awful lot. An entire shopping trolley of them. To get the spuds back to our offices required stealing the shopping trolley and wheeling it down Tottenham Court Road. The problem was that Tottenham Court Road was crammed to capacity with crazed, wild-eyed people frenziedly doing their Christmas shopping. Standing room only. We could barely force our way through. Coupled with that, the trolley kept making bids for freedom, veering madly out of control and threatening to upend itself into the gutter.

At about six o'clock, everyone was decked out in their party frocks and high heels (even some of the women) and everything was ready.

Except the sheep.

The weather in London wasn't quite as clement as in the foothills of the Atlas mountains. It had started to snow lightly down on top of the sheep so Ahmed's fire kept going out. Also it seemed that he wasn't as *au fait* with the roasting of entire sheep as he'd let on, and had miscalculated the amount of time needed to cook them. By about twelve hours.

All one hundred and fifty staff repaired to the upstairs bar, where a combination of hunger, exhaustion, anticipation and a free bar for an hour meant that, in a commendably short time, everyone was *twisted*. Later that evening, the shout went up that dinner was served. But as everyone else stampeded down the stairs for their bit of raw sheep, I remained in the bar, slumped on the sofa with my friend Louise. I was too wrecked from my day of peeling carrots and wrestling with shopping trollies to go anywhere. There were only two other people left in the bar. A woman and a mad old academic with a floppy, polka-dotted bow-tie and a great fondness for the sauce. They were both scuttered. At the best of times me laddo wasn't too steady on his pins and needed a walking stick to get around. But he was so jarred he could hardly stand as he left to make his way down the stairs, assisted by his woman-friend who was nearly as bad as him. Lurching and leaning on each other, they made it to the door of the bar, then disappeared round the doorway to descend the stairs. Louise and I were poised for it. We stopped our conversation and held our breath. And sure enough, within seconds, we heard it. The rhythmic bumpity, bumpity, bumpity bump of a pissed academic with arthritic knees falling down the stairs, ricocheting between wall and bannister as he went. There followed a short, expectant pause, a kind of pregnant silence, and we concluded that he had arrived at the little landing halfway down. Again we held our breath, then exhaled with relief as the bumpity, bumpity, bumpity bump began again, as he tumbled down the second half of the stairs, concluding with a satisfying crack as he obviously hit his head on the slate floor at the bottom.

I'm sorry, but we laughed. We laughed till we cried. We clutched each other and nearly puked from laughing. It had been a long, exhausting day, but all the same that's no excuse. When the spasms of merriment eventually passed and we could walk, we went and had a look over the bannisters. The academic was sprawled on the floor at the bottom, being revived – the way you should with extremely drunk people – by a glass of white wine administered by his bollocksed lady-friend. He was surrounded by a ring of people only marginally less jarred than himself, who were offering all kinds of conflicting advice. Stand him up. Don't move him. Ask him who the Prime Minister is. Don't be bothering him. Give him brandy. Get his stomach pumped. There was talk of calling an ambulance.

'He might have brain damage,' someone said.

'Would anyone notice?' one wag asked.

Eventually, they managed to agree that an ambulance wasn't necessary, that he was good and mad already. A taxi was called for instead, and he, his walking stick and his glass of wine were carried as far as the car. While he was helped in, someone placed his glass of wine on the roof of the cab. Then, as the disgruntled taxi-driver screeched away from the kerb with his scuttered cargo, the glass of wine was sent flying off the roof, spattering the well-wishers with sweet, sticky Liebfraumilch.

God, those were the days . . .

First published in *Irish Tatler*, December 1998.

Happy Christmas! Form an Orderly Queue

*C*hristmas. Be afraid. Be very afraid. Allegedly the season of goodwill to all men, anyone with a bit of sense knows that it's anything but.

Christmas is about waking up seventeen mornings in a row swearing that tonight really *will* be the night that you go to bed before two a.m. It's about battling through brightly lit, over-heated department stores, sweating in your coat, scarf and gloves. It's about breaking the mini-sausage-roll of peace with your boss at the office party, drinking vast quantities of Piat d'Or from white plastic cups, then a couple of hours later pushing people out of the way in your haste to photocopy your bottom.

It's about hordes of Irish people coming home from abroad, being welcomed by their overjoyed parents at Dublin airport, then saying awkwardly, 'Thanks for coming, but . . . ah, listen . . . I said I'd go straight into town to meet Malachy and Annie and the others, so sorry about that. Er, but as you've come all this way, no point in you having a wasted journey, any chance you'd drop me into town and take my bags home with you?'

It's about queueing for several days to get a taxi, it's about watching the fisticuffs break out at Midnight Mass, it's about drunkenly wrapping your presents late on Christmas Eve, then being mortified when you see what a hames you made of it, in the cold, sober light of Christmas morning.

But above all, Christmas is about rows. Terrible rows. Shocking, unexpected rows. Caused partly by the huge gap between the expectations of Christmas and what it actually delivers. And partly by there being too many self-governing, autonomous adults crammed into one house, having to obey someone else's rules and follow someone else's routine. (I also blame the central heating being up too high.)

I used to think I was the only person who had big scraps over the festive period, but now that I've opened up about my secret shame, I find it's going on everywhere.

But there are some good things about Christmas, of course. Presents!

Since time immemorial, every Christmas morning my four siblings and I had to queue up outside the locked door of the front room. Waiting for the glorious moment when our mother would turn the key and we would be propelled as one into the room, to fall with glad cries on the Scalextric, Tiny Tears, Polly Pockets and other delights within.

Mam is a real showman and would drag the unlocking out as long as possible. Meanwhile, we squirmed in an agony of anticipation, until the five of us were concertinaed into the space that one person normally filled. The idea was to have the oldest in front one year and the youngest the following, which was fair to everyone except the child in the middle.

This practice continued well into our adult lives. But of course, once alcohol was introduced into the equation, the landscape of Christmas morning altered irrevocably. Inconceivable though it would once have seemed, it suddenly became more important for some family members to lie in bed roaring for a basin than to be queueing outside the front room shouting 'No pushing at the back!'

And no matter how pitifully the younger members pleaded to be admitted without their hungover siblings, my mother was firm. All or nothing. Until every single one of the five of us was present the door wouldn't be opened.

Desperate measures were called for. A couple of them went outside in their bare feet and pyjamas and tried to look past the impenetrable barrier of the lace curtains of the front room to see if they could catch a glimpse of something within that looked like a My Little Pony.

'Can you see anything moving in there?' asked Tadhg anxiously, who spent his entire childhood vainly hoping to be given a dog. (When he dies, the inscription on his tombstone will read 'Can we get a dog, Mam? Can we Mam? Can we?')

Back into the house to search frantically for an electric cattle prod all the better to hasten the rising of the lie-a-bed offenders. None to be found. Nothing doing but to burst into the hungover person's room, brutally turn on the light, stand at the foot of their bed and shriek, 'Get up, you selfish pig!'

'Carry on without me, men,' groaned the bedbound lush. 'I'll only slow you down.'

'Just get up for five minutes,' someone else reasoned. 'Then when we've been let in you can go straight back to bed.'

That usually worked. But instead of entering the room like

a bullet out of a gun, as we used to, it was a small army of walking wounded that shuffled forward lacklustrely to open their packets of gift-wrapped pot pourri.

Ah, pot pourri! Where would we be without it? It says so much. It says, I don't know you very well, but am obliged because of circumstances to give you something. It's the kind of thing sisters-in-law give each other. The perfect present for your father's girlfriend or your colleagues. At Christmas, I don't think of the star in the east leading the three wise men or of the little baby being born in a stable. Instead I bow my head and am humbled by the thought of so many gift-wrapped parcels of pot pourri changing hands.

But of course, Christmas isn't just about presents and materialistic things. Christmas is about so much more than that. Christmas is about food.

Lots and lots and lots of food.

I devote myself to it with almost mystic zeal, trying to barricade myself into my bedroom with tins of Chocolate Kimberleys. I am truly disgusting and I get so caught up in the terrible gluttony of it all that I'm not able to do anything else. Every Stephen's Day for the past ten years, my sister Caitríona, my friend Eileen and I have made noises about going to the races. I have yet to achieve it.

'Are you coming to the races?' Caitríona demands, while I lie in bed.

'I can't,' I mumble, my mouth full of Crunchies. 'I've set myself a challenge. I'm going for a personal best on the selection-box eating.'

'Fair enough,' she says. 'Well, the best of luck, do you want me to time you?'

For a moment a cold hand of fear clutches my heart as I think of all the starving and exercise I'll have to do in January. But that bleak, hairshirt month seems a long way away. I'll deal with it when it happens.

'Get the stopwatch!' I command. 'I feel lucky.'

First published in *Irish Tatler*, December 1997.

A Quiet Millennium Night In

Few events in the past decade have generated as much discussion as the question of what you'd be doing on the night that the new millennium dawned. This is a piece I wrote for Irish Tatler *about what I'd planned for it.*

The world is divided in two. Not along the lines of people who have inny and people who have outy belly buttons, but between those (like myself) who abhor New Year's Eve and those who love it. If you're one of those people who think New Year's Eve is '*Great* fun!' then please stop reading now. You'll only think I'm a whingy misery guts. But if you're the kind of person who, even as you screech 'Happy New Year!' with eighty other revellers, feels a black hole of bleakness corroding within you, then read on.

New Year's Eve tips me into the worst pit of depression of the entire year. I inadvertently stray into a negative twilight zone where I take stock of my life and find it very, very lacking. No matter how happy I am the other 364 days of the year, I suddenly feel like a horrible, lonely failure the night before the New Year arrives. The rest of the year I know I'm not that bad, but all positive thought is washed away by whatever bad energy is abroad on New Year's Eve.

Not only that, but whatever I plan for the night never really works out. As the clock strikes midnight, heralding the arrival of the New Year, I'm either:

a) being refused entry to a party;
b) traipsing around a housing estate looking for a party which doesn't exist;
c) part of the mass exodus of over-refreshed zombies streaming out of town, night-of-the-living-dead style, looking for a taxi;
d) nose to nose in a shockingly unexpected shouting match with my nearest and dearest;
e) in bed, feigning 'flu.

So as I've never made any secret of my dislike of the *regular* New Year's Eve, can you imagine how much more of a loser I'm going to feel *this* year when the whole song and dance will be magnified to the power of . . . well . . . two thousand?

For the last eighteen months there's been no escape. The question of where you're going to be when the third millennium dawns has been passionately discussed in pubs and around dinner tables and at bus stops everywhere. In fact, it's overtaken 'will Tom and Nicole's marriage last?' as that handy conversation filler when you end up sitting next to the world's most boring man at a work thing.

But while the rest of the world has been talking about seeing in the new millennium by flying to Fiji or getting a house in Bundoran or paying two hundred and fifty quid for steak and chips and a thousand quid for a babysitter, I've been Mrs Killjoy. Though I've tried to keep a lid on my curmudgeonliness, sometimes I just can't stop myself from offering a choice of five responses. Which are as follows. 'So we're celebrating the 2,000 years since the birth of Christ? Well:

a) He didn't exist.
b) Or if he did exist he was born 2,004 years ago.
c) Even if he was born 2,000 years ago, I thought the *25th* of December was his birthday.
d) We haven't reached 2,000 years until the end of the 2,000 years, i.e. *next* New Year's Eve.
e) It's only because we have ten fingers that we think this is significant. If, for example, we had nine fingers we'd count in base nine and the year 2,000 would have been in 1458.'

That usually puts paid to any discussion, I always find.

But I've recently discovered that I'm not the only person in the world who finds New Year's Eve a trial. There are others like me. Oh yes! And we've decided to stop suffering in silence. My friend Aoife says she's hardly ever had a nice New Year's Eve, that something horrible usually happened, like going to a party and seeing the fella she fancied get off with someone else. To which my friend Suzanne chipped in and said that Aoife was lucky, that at least she'd managed to *find* the party.

Anyway, to make a long story slightly not so long, what I decided to do was provide a safe house. A safe haven for those with New Year's fear and especially for those with New Millennium's fear. Anyone who wanted could come to my house for an Alternative Newer. Himself and myself decided we'd hide all the clocks, so no one would know when it was twelve o'clock. For the same reason, we wouldn't have the telly on. Instead we decided to show Audrey Hepburn movies – *Roman Holiday, Funny Face, Breakfast at Tiffany's*. We'd keep all the curtains firmly drawn so as not to be bothered by bloody fireworks, and if the local church bells started pealing like mad, we'd pretend it was just an extended version of the Angelus.

Naturally, we'd get in a ton of food and drink, but instead of having to sip your champagne and balance a small plate of cocktail sausages and mini-pizzas while making polite conversation, we decreed that you could consume your food and drink any way you liked at our party – sullenly thrown on the couch, swigging straight from the bottle, cramming Pringle after Pringle into one's mouth if so desired. As people arrived they'd be frisked at the door and relieved of any silly hats, whistles, sprigs of mistletoe and other wacky New Year's Eve paraphernalia, and anyone bursting into a spontaneous chorus of 'TEN! NINE! EIGHT! SEVEN! –' would be gently but firmly ejected. And the same thing would happen to anyone who went around upsetting the other guests by asking them what they were giving up for the new millennium.

When I mentioned the idea of the safe house to others, the response I got was incredible. Some people looked at me as if I was insane and called me a miserable cow, but others loved it and even added some wonderful contributions of their own. One friend suggested having a roomful of duvets, so when the existential angst became too much, we could wrap ourselves up, curl into a foetal ball, rock back and forth and make gentle keening noises. And I have to say that of all the facilities on offer that evening, this proved one of the most popular.

Anyway, the whole lovely thing has gone pear-shaped. My sister in New York got wind of it and rang me with the ominous words, 'What about this open house you're having on New Year's Eve?'

'Not an *open* house,' I gently corrected her. 'It's a *safe* house.'

There followed a horrible pause and I had a hair-standing-on-the-back-of-my-neck presentiment of disaster. 'Safe house?' she said cheerfully. 'Not any more.'

It turned out that she'd invited some people. Quite a few people. People who had no interest in rolling around in duvets, unless it was with a member of the opposite sex and four bottles of champagne. People who wanted to party. People who planned to start shouting 'TEN! NINE! EIGHT! SEVEN! –' several days before the off.

Every phone call from her brings more news. She's bought a floor-length frock, with diamanté shoulder straps for the night that's in it. Her friend Louise is after acquiring a load of furry toys which, when wound up, shout the countdown in squeaky voices, then dance and wish everyone a Happy New Year. There's been talk of tiaras, which apparently everyone *must* wear. By all accounts she's organized a posse to descend on the house to festoon it with appropriate millennial decorations on the day. And allegedly no party is complete without a fireworks display in the garden.

Over the past month I've bumped into people I know only vaguely who've thanked me for inviting them to the party-to-end-all-parties on New Year's Eve. One of them asked me how we were going to manage the link-up.

'What link-up?' I asked, scarcely able to believe my ears.

The person shrugged. 'I dunno, really, but she said something about a radio link-up with New York.'

Strangely, my initial horror has calmed and my sister has progressively eroded my objections to the point where I'm looking forward to it now. Well, sort of ... So, Happy New Millennium! (Even though it's an entirely meaningless concept, as the starting date was simply an arbitrary point in history, yadda, yadda.)

First published in *Irish Tatler*, January 2000.

BOTH SIDES OF THE
IRISH SEA

I left Ireland in 1986 and moved to London. I thought I would stay there for ever. Which just goes to show. In 1997 I moved back to Dublin and love it.

Swinging London

*F*ourteen years ago, I left my middle-class suburban home in Dublin and escaped to London. Back then Dublin wasn't the booming, open-minded, latte-ridden, cosmopolitan place that it is today. 'This is a one-horse town,' I taunted my mother. 'And that horse is a Catholic fundamentalist.' Then I added moodily, 'No one understands me. Just wait till I get to London.' Teenage angst is an ugly thing, especially in a twenty-two-year-old.

So off I went on the boat and train, like thousands had done before me. The only thing was, I was different, or so I'd have you believe. I'd had the benefit of an education and I wasn't coming to London looking for work, I was coming looking for shoes. And clothes. I'd heard a rumour (true, as it happened) that Bodymap (very big in 1986) had a stall at Camden Market where seconds were sold cheap. And I arrived at Euston station at six a.m., one perishing February morning, looking for the balm of anonymity – I suspected that no one belonged in London, so I stood the same chance as everyone else of fitting in. Even at that horribly early hour I noticed that Dublin had existed for me in black and white while London was decked out in all-singing, all-dancing glorious technicolour.

The bag I'd brought was almost unliftable – I'd packed every stitch I possessed and some of Caitríona's stitches too, because I knew London was a trendy, stylish place and I didn't want to let myself down. As well as shoes and clothes, I had high hopes of finding lots of men in London. Dublin was so small that all eligible men had been catalogued and bagged, but London seemed a teeming mass of untapped potential. My motto was, There are no strangers, only ex-boyfriends I haven't met yet.

My poor father obviously had an inkling of this, because he'd taken me aside and given me an oblique lecture before I left – much talk of 'shop-soiled goods' and 'secondhand cars' and how most men like to play with but don't like to marry them. 'Understand?' he asked anxiously.

'Certainly, Dad. Why would any man want to marry a secondhand car?'

And his well-meaning advice fell on barren ground, because no sooner was I off the train at Euston station than I moved in with my friend Conor. Conor was a man (this was very bad) who happened to be gay (my Dad was torn – he couldn't decide if this made it better or worse), and the flat happened to be a squat, on the twenty-first floor of a tower block in Hackney. We had almost no furniture and one cup, which was available to me on a rota basis.

Disasters started to happen to me and I embraced them joyously. I felt that I was living, truly alive for the first time in my life. On my first day as a citizen of Hackney, a Genghis Khan lookalike, his sixteen-inch meat cleaver and his hungry Alsatian joined me in the lift. They both snarled at me until the seventeenth floor, when they politely got out.

On my second day, a man flashed at me on the Tube. You wouldn't get that happening to you in holy Catholic Ireland, I swaggered.

On my third day, I got stuck in the lift for an hour and a half and was liberated by firemen, who had to come down the liftshaft, remove the roof of the cage and hoist me out. I was passed like the lightest football from hunky fireman to hunky fireman until I was back on terra firma. Conor almost wept with jealousy and accused me of staging it.

Everything and everywhere was exciting. I met so many people, from all over. Leicester and Glasgow, Brighton and Cardiff, Leeds and Taunton, Jamaica and Canada. Not too many native Londoners, though. I bought myself a Bodymap frock (red, tight, hole cut out in the thigh) and a black, sealskin coat in Kensington Market, and I reckoned I cut a fairly impressive dash on the dance-floors of Taboo and Heaven. (The only people I knew in London were gay; I became a fag-hag by default.) I had boundless energy and partied all night. Then got the night-bus home to sleep most of the day, waking at five in the evening for a breakfast of toast and Dairylea.

Some days we roused ourselves in time to go and stroke sweaters in expensive clothes shops. Conor was well up on all kinds of names that I'd never heard before — Valentino, Joseph, Azzedine Alaia. He'd bring me into a small, bare emporium and stand in tearful reverence before a tight, white, double-lycra dress.

Another day he took me to the King's Road and I was overwhelmed by the iconic nature of what I was doing. I *insisted* on buying something – after all, it wasn't every day that a girl from Ireland got to go down the King's Road. And I *did* buy something – a chicken breast from Safeway, for my tea.

Escaping from parental control and what I felt was the goldfish-bowl syndrome of Ireland was immensely liberating. I could be anyone I wanted to be. Hell, I could even be myself. I made full use of the fact that I no longer had anyone breathing down my neck to go to Mass. Every Sunday was spent savouring the freedom of Not Going To Mass. And I could do the Walk of Shame anytime I wanted in London and no one turned a blind eye. Whereas in Dublin if I'd returned home at seven in the morning, wearing last night's clothes, my knickers in my pocket, I was convinced it'd get on the evening news.

On the rare occasions that I rang home, my mother always enquired tearfully, 'Have you a job yet?' 'No, Mam,' I boasted. Then, bursting with pride, I outlined the current state of play. 'I. Am. On. The. Dole.'

'Oh Sacred Heart of Jesus,' she muttered and I knew she was blessing herself. 'You're able-bodied and you've an education and what if you get caught? And have you any furniture in that . . . whatever it is . . . *skip* you're living in.'

'It's a squat, and yes we have. We have an armchair, which I'm allowed to sit in when Conor isn't around.'

Vaguely, I toyed with the idea of looking for a job. Unlike Ireland, where there were literally no jobs, London was bursting with an abundance of them. And I was in the privileged position of having a degree in law. But my few forays into employment agencies yielded little fruit. And even fewer job interviews. A degree was no bad thing, seemed to be the general consensus. Better than, say, a criminal record. But a degree from an *Irish* university wasn't regarded as much cop. I wasn't disappointed, I wasn't even surprised. I wouldn't have had it any other way, to be honest. After all, I'd grown up in the shadow of Britain, where everything in Ireland was regarded as a second-rate version of the British equivalent. The only thing we'd ever given to the world which the world had seemed to want was Irish coffee. Our pop groups were toe-cringingly derivative, our few magazines were low-rent rip-offs, even our slang seemed shamefully poor – why would anyone in their right mind ever ask 'How's it going?' when they could enquire, with an *EastEnders* inflection, 'Alright?' (Of course, I know things are very different today, when there is no greater hipness than to be Irish – actors, stand-up comedians, writers, pop groups instantly acquire a sexy, whimsical charm the minute they lay their hands on their Irish roots. If you'd told me then what it would be like today, I would have felt really sorry for you.)

So when I'd been shown the door by yet another employment agency, I felt I could relax with impunity into my life of bohemian, state-sponsored indolence. It went on for a few more fun-filled months, however all good things come to an end. Middle-class guilt coupled with Irish Catholic guilt is a fairly irresistible combination, and eventually all that not working and enjoying myself took its toll. I *had* to get a job and actually, when it came down to it, there wasn't that much available to me. I couldn't type, my accent wasn't the right one for a receptionist, and unfortunately I wasn't a man so I couldn't become a brickie.

In the absence of any other opportunities I became a waitress, and actually I had a whale of a time. I was young and energetic, and doing menial work still had great novelty value. It was the matt-black eighties where people flung money around like snuff at a wake. Tips rained down on me, even though I was possibly the worst waitress *ever* to fling burgers in front of people. Other waitresses could carry a dozen laden plates up each arm. The most I could manage was two. In total, that is. Other waitresses remembered to bring customers their drinks. I didn't. Other waitresses managed not to spill hot-pepper sauce on to customers. I didn't.

On account of my waitressing skills, I was promoted. To the office. To do the sums. Despite hating maths at school, I appeared to have a strange aptitude for accounts work. Lo and behold, it seemed that despite my best efforts I had somehow got respectable. I railed against my new image for a while, but the gig was up. Surrendering to my fate, I said goodbye to the squat and moved into a flat which had more than one cup and where I was required to pay rent.

But that wasn't the end of the adventure. Oh no, that was just the start of it . . .

First published in *Cara* magazine, November 2000.

Do You Know the Bus Stop in Kilkenny?

When I was living in London, I was misfortunate enough
to work with someone who loved to ridicule the illogicality of the Irish. He regularly came into my office and did
diddley-idle impressions of Irish people giving directions.
Stuff along the lines of 'Do you know where the road forks
to the left? You do? Good! Well, don't go that way. Go past
the house that used to have the yellow door, past where
Murphy's shop used to be before they knocked it down. And
when you get to the end of the road and there's a pub at the
bottom of it, you've gone the wrong way, but so what, you
might as well have a drink, anyway.'

'You Oirish!' he'd wheeze, doubled over with mirth.
'You're so daft.'

'Ha ha,' I used to deadpan. 'Stop, you're killing me.' Then
I would file his expenses claim in the paper shredder, or
'mistakenly' put him on the most savage tax code known to
mankind, or manage it so that he was tragically omitted from
the monthly payroll. Working in an accounts office can have
its small yet intensely pleasurable compensations. (Paydays
were an especial joy – the building echoing with screams of
gibbering terror as an offender opened his payslip to find his

take-home pay was a big fat zero.) But since I've moved back from London to live in Dublin, I have to admit that my colleague might have had a bit of a point – and that it's no bad thing either. Giving directions is an *art form* in Ireland.

For example, if a Londoner invites you to visit them at their home, naturally enough you'll ask them where they live. And they'll reply – let's just say – 'Jefferson Road, in Fulham,' or 'Shirland Road, in Maida Vale.' Efficient and effective.

In Ireland, however, it's a different kettle of fish. Shortly after I moved back, a native of Dublin invited me to his home. And when I asked where he lived, instead of saying Marlborough Road in Donnybrook – which is what his address was – he replied obliquely, 'Do you know the taxi rank in Ranelagh?'

'Yes,' I said, wondering what it had to do with where he lived.

'Let me see,' he said thoughtfully, his eyes narrowed to help him visualize. 'As you're coming out of town . . . now hold on a while! Will you be driving or getting the bus or walking?'

I said that I wasn't sure yet, that I wouldn't be sure until I knew where exactly it was that he lived . . .

'We'll pretend for the minute that you're driving,' he interrupted. 'OK, as you're coming out of town, the taxi rank is on your right. Go past the flower shop. Do you know the flower shop? Just past the taxi rank?'

I didn't. And I suggested that if he gave me the number and name of his road, I could look it up on the map and there was no need for these directions . . .

'Well, do you know the Spar in Ranelagh then?' he said, ignoring me.

'Yes, but . . .'

That pleased him, but when I once again made reference to a map, his derision was excoriating. 'A *map!*' he laughed scornfully. 'What do you want a map for? Where do you think this is? The foothills of the Himalayas? Right, do you know the dry-cleaner's in Ranelagh? Just past the flower shop?'

When I'd resignedly admitted to knowing the dry-cleaner's, the chipper, the pizza take-away place, the chemist, Burchills the pub and most of the other businesses in Ranelagh, his face suddenly clouded over with doubt. 'Of course, you could do this a completely different way,' he said. 'Do you know the bus garage in Donnybrook?'

A few days later it happened again. I was going to see an old schoolfriend who was married and living in suburban affluence somewhere in the Raheny area. 'Give me your address,' I said firmly. 'And I'll look it up on the map.'

'Right,' she said agreeably. 'Do you know Fairview Park?' She then took me through the three-mile journey from Fairview to Raheny, navigating with reference to almost every pub, chipper and SuperValu *en route*.

But it was alright. By then I'd become completely Irish again. It had taken a couple of days to settle back in, but I was firing on all Hibernian cylinders once more. Well into what my colleague in London called Irish illogicality and what I call Irish lyricism.

Giving people detailed directions is all part of Irish hospitality. Expecting people to find their way with a map is tantamount to inviting people to dinner and expecting them to bring their own food. Which is why an Irish person can almost never say 'I don't know,' when asked for directions. In the same way that they'd give the visitor all their food and do without themselves, they'd rather say something – *anything* – than say nothing.

Which can sometimes bring about interesting results. Take the bank holiday Monday last October when the Dublin City Marathon was on. Myself and Himself were walking down Baggot Street and we encountered a few of the marathon participants panting and heaving themselves towards us. From their accents and their giant T-shirts proclaiming 'Milwaukee Dentists', we deduced that they were Americans. They were loudly complaining that the directions for the marathon were hopeless. 'Which way do we go now?' they demanded of each other, looking at the canal. I hadn't a notion, but I was quite happy to stop so that they could have a good complain at me. When out of nowhere a voice shouted, 'Left. Go left!'

We all turned to see a benign-smiling, flushed-of-face, pint-holding man standing in the doorway of the pub by the canal.

'Hey, thanks!' the runners yelled, their faces beaming, obviously deeply charmed by this human signpost, this stranger taking an interest in their welfare. Instantly they were mentally tearing up all the letters of complaint they'd written in their heads. Instead they were rehearsing the glowing praise they'd heap when they got back home – 'In our city we got computerized signboards, but in Eyorland they got *real people*.' Whooping and 'Way to go'ing and 'Nice piece of work'ing and generally being Americans, they burst into a sprint along the canal.

'I don't think it's left,' Himself muttered to me. 'I think that man has sent them the wrong way.' There was no point berating Himself for not entering the 'Which way to go' debate. After all, he's English and middle class and is therefore genetically incapable of giving directions to total strangers without first having being formally introduced. Instead, I turned to the man in the doorway. 'Are you sure it's left?' I anxiously asked him.

He gave me an aggrieved look. 'Sure, I had to say *something*,' he said defensively.

The poor Yanks are probably still running.

First published in *Irish Tatler*, April 1998.

The Early Bird ... Catches the Host on the Hop

*I*t's a while since I moved back to Ireland, after living in England for eleven years. A big move, further complicated by the fact that on my return to the Emerald Isle, I imported Himself, an Englishman. Though he's highly pro-Irish, naturally enough I worried that he might get homesick, so I resolved to monitor closely his car-washing, DIY and other acts of Englishness. Secure in the knowledge that if his yearning for his homeland got really out of hand there was somewhere I could send him to — a small part of Ireland that will remain for ever England. I speak not of the six counties in the North, but, of course, of the Jervis Street Shopping Centre.

'Leave that shelf,' I'd say. 'You've put up enough, we're running out of wall. Go on off and have a wander around Boots, Argos, Dixons, Debenhams, Waterstones and all the rest, and pretend you're perambulating the highways and byways of Hemel Hempstead. Get everything out of your system! Have a pot of Earl Grey while you're out there and don't come back until you're happy again to be living in Ireland.' It invariably worked, and Englishman usually came back all aglow, having overheard some strange Irish phrase that caught his fancy. 'What does "Take it handy" mean?

What exactly is an oul' segosha? Animal, vegetable or mineral?'

As for myself, the thing that I was most worried about on my return from exile was the goldfish-bowlness of Ireland. The way if you sneeze in Tara Street, by the time you get off the Dart in Dun Laoghaire, someone will ask you how your cold is. And it didn't matter how much people boasted that Ireland was highly sophisticated and cosmopolitan now, that very often you could be living next door to someone for – ooh – could be up to *two weeks* without being invited in for a cup of tea, I wasn't convinced.

Sure enough, within days of moving into our new house, I was on my way down to the post office when I was accosted by a woman I didn't know from a bar of soap. 'I was passing your house and that was a perfectly good breadbin you threw out there,' she greeted me with. '*Perfectly* good. Any charity would have been delighted with it. Criminal waste, that's what it is. *Criminal.*' Against all expectation, instead of wanting to tell her to shag off and mind her own business, I was strangely touched. In London it seems people don't care if it's dismembered bodies you're throwing out, just so long as they don't have to make eye contact with you. I found myself explaining how the breadbin had managed to contract some superhuman strain of mould that no amount of scrubbing would shift. 'I'd have appreciated the chance to find out,' she said wistfully, flexing her hands. I assured her that the next time she would. Now I bump into her regularly and her opening gambit is always something like, 'I see you were away for a couple of days there. Cork, I believe?' Or 'What was in the parcel you got from Germany? It looked like books but I couldn't be certain.' I haven't a clue how she manages to monitor me so thoroughly – despite my beady-eyed surveillance, I've never once been able to spot her lying in the hedge with her long-range lens. I love meeting her, she knows so much about me that there's always a chance I'll find out some surprise information about myself. When I couldn't find my last-year's swimming togs, I nearly asked her if she knew where I'd left them.

But what I appreciate most about living in Ireland is the Random Visitor Factor. For people who've never lived in London, it's hard to understand what a big banana is made of house calls there. Visits are arranged months in advance and because of the vast distances to be covered they're treated like a great race migration. Nobody just 'drops in'. Nobody but weirdos, that is. With the result that if the doorbell ever rang unexpectedly, my flatmates and I used to look at each other in horror. 'Hide!' was the customary reaction. Although more often than not it just turned out to be a pizza delivery at the wrong address.

But here, if the bell rings unexpectedly, it's exciting. There's always the chance that it's not the itinerants. (Although there's a very good chance that it *is* the itinerants. News of Himself has obviously spread far and wide through the travelling community. He's forever coming in from the door, shaking his head and saying things like, 'It's very sad. The man who was just at the door, his mother has died and he didn't even have the fare to her funeral. And what a coincidence! That's the fifth person today with the same problem. And who would have thought that train fares to Galway would be so expensive? C'mere, have you any money? They've cleaned me out.')

And not only do we get visitors, but we're also invited to people's homes, and I'm afraid this is the one area of our reintegration that Himself and myself fall down on. See, the way it is in England, if someone says to be at their flat for dinner at seven-thirty, what they mean is you're to come at twenty to eight. But in Ireland, if someone says to be at their flat for dinner at seven-thirty, what they mean is you're to come at a quarter past nine. At the earliest. I knew this, at least I *thought* I did. So the first time we were invited to an Irish person's home for our evening meal, I insisted that we be a full half-hour late – while Himself frenziedly pawed the ground and champed at the bit and begged to be allowed to get going. And when we arrived neither the host nor hostess was home from work yet.

The fifteen anxious minutes spent waiting in the car taught us a hard lesson, so the next time we were invited out we were an entire hour late. And arrived just in time to get the woman out of the shower. Dripping, she came down the stairs in her dressing-gown and told us which cupboard in the kitchen we could find the Hula Hoops in. I was mortified, I'd never felt so anal in all my life.

But I'm getting better. I've worked my way up to being an hour and a half late, and God willing, I'm hoping it won't be too long before I can manage an entire two hours. And then all traces of my time in England will have disappeared. You'd nearly think I'd never left Ireland at all.

First published in *Irish Tatler*, May 1999.

Psycho Magnet

Since I've passed my driving test I don't go on public transport so often, which is a terrible shame.

Something strange happened to me on a Thursday night recently. It was about eleven o'clock and I was waiting to get the bus from Blackrock in the suburbs into the middle of the great metropolis of Dublin. I waited the regulation twenty minutes and wondered why it wasn't raining. Eventually, a bus turned the corner and lumbered towards me. It was a number 45, the bus that plies the route between Bray, Co. Wicklow and the city of Dublin, and I marvelled in wonder. You don't see these beasts often, they're almost like 46As in their shyness and elusiveness. (A sure sign that someone is going bananas is when they often talk about getting 46As.)

I flagged it down and, to my great surprise, it stopped. My experience is that Dublin bus-drivers have a great sense of 'fun'. And nothing is as much 'fun' as speeding right past a bus stop full of people who've been waiting half an hour in the freezing cold, leaving them staring after the bus in outrage, the sounds of the bus-driver's hysterical laughter and 'Yiz poor eejits, if yiz could only see yer faces!' floating in its wake.

On I clambered. Because I wasn't sure what the exact fare was (I would normally get the 46A), I just waved money in the driver's general direction and said, 'Town, please.' The driver had a slightly hunted air about him, and said, 'How much do you normally pay?'

'I don't know,' I replied. 'I don't often come this route.'

'Usually go on the 46A?' he asked, giving me a funny look. 'OK, give me a pound and we'll call it quits.'

I didn't give this exchange a moment's thought. I'm used to the I-make-it-up-as-I-go-along approach of Dublin bus-drivers to their fare schedule. About a week before, for three days in a row I was charged three different fares for exactly the same route. On day one I was charged £1.10, so the next day I proffered £1.10 only to have 10p returned to me. On day three I handed over £1.00, only to be berated for trying to swizz the driver and didn't everyone know the fare was £1.20? I find this spontaneous method of pricing charming and quirky. (Except when they shout at me and embarrass me in front of the whole bus.)

On the Thursday night in question, the bus was almost empty, just one other passenger on the lower deck. I sat down and began to read my book, and moments later the woman who was the other passenger got out of her seat and came to sit beside me. 'I'm scared,' she said.

My heart sank. Not again.

I am some kind of looper magnet. It doesn't happen to anyone else I know. But poor, tormented, demented people seem to find me a kindred spirit. I simply cannot make a journey on public transport without being joined by a lunatic. (And I'm not just talking about the times I get the bus with Himself.)

This is what usually happens. Picture the scene: the top deck of a bus, only one passenger on it (me), sitting quietly, reading her book, bothering no one. Up the stairs lurches another person. They look around, survey all forty-three empty seats, and decide that the nicest one of all is the one that's right next to me. They plump themselves down not so much next to me as *on* me, their left thigh entirely obscuring my right one, my shoulder dislocating itself against the glass from the weight of their body pushing against me. Usually they seem to have dispensed with the rudiments of personal hygiene, if the ripe aroma that emanates from them is anything to go by.

And then it starts. 'They're all spies, you know,' they tell me. If I've heard that once I've heard it a thousand times. Or 'They're trying to bleed my brain, they're sending messages through the plug sockets.' Or 'I see spaceships landing in my neighbour's garden every Monday night.' Or 'They're trying to brainwash me through the lamp-posts.' Etc, etc.

'I'm scared,' the woman said again. I turned to look at her – at least as much as I could because she was so close to me there wasn't much room for manoeuvring – and she didn't look too bad. She was probably in her forties and had a scrubbed, innocent little face that I took as proof positive that she was round the bend. No normal person would look so *shiny*. But she was dressed conventionally enough. She wasn't barefoot or wearing a dinner jacket over her nightdress like the last one I'd had.

'Why are you scared?' I asked, and braced myself for talk of spies, brainwashing and plug sockets.

'It's the driver,' she whispered. 'He's going very fast, and he's going all the wrong way.' I made soothing noises, because even though I wished she'd go away and let me read my book, I couldn't help but sympathize with her. While I hadn't exactly ever been in the 'I see spaceships in my neighbour's garden' category, there were times when I'd been laid so low with the depression that I was fully convinced I was losing my marbles.

'He drove through Monkstown Village, you know,' she confided in a little-girl voice. 'And that's not on the route, sure it isn't.' Indeed it wasn't, and I marvelled at the colourfulness and the detail of her delusions.

'I don't think he's a real driver,' she told me quietly. 'I think he's an impostor.'

'I suppose you think he's a spy,' I said kindly, keen to let her know I was on her side.

She drew back from me sharply. 'A *spy*?' she hooted. 'Why would I think that?' She studied me carefully. 'Are you all right?'

She was obviously having a moment of lucidity, I realized. It often happened. For the duration of my journey we sat in uncomfortable silence, wedged shoulder to shoulder, while other passengers got on and off.

What felt like a long, long time later, my stop finally

approached. I murmured 'Excuse me' to the scaredy cat and wriggled past her to get out. As I stood in the aisle waiting for the bus to stop, there was a glamorous, short-skirted, blonde-haired wan ahead of me, undeniably *en route* to a wild night out. In the midst of my usual pang that I'd never again get away with wearing a skirt as short as hers, I overheard her having a conversation with the bus-driver. 'Do you go down Nassau Street?' she asked.

Even though he was rattling at very high speed past Merrion Square, he took his eyes off the road to flick her a haunted, beseiged look. 'I don't know,' he said, in a hoarse, panicky voice. 'I don't know the names of any of the roads. I don't know the fares. I keep losing my way and going off the route. I'm only new.'

I turned around and looked at the shiny-faced woman. Suddenly she looked very, very normal and I felt very, very ashamed.

First published in *Irish Tatler*, March 1998.

Slacking Off is Hard to Do

*B*lah, blah, blah, Celtic Tiger ... blah, blah, house prices ... blah, traffic gridlock ... blah, working very hard.

At the moment there's such a great wealth of opportunities available in Ireland that anyone with a job is going round hollow-eyed and exhausted. From cleaners to pensions analysts, we're *wrecked*. I'm not complaining. Well, I'm not *exactly* complaining. I was one of the 50,000 who emigrated in 1986 looking for work and it's great that we have more than enough work to go round. And yet, and yet ... I can't help thinking of the old days, the old art forms. Like Dossing at Work. Will its likes never be here again?

Does anyone remember the days when you'd arrive fifteen minutes late, take another fifteen minutes to drink a cup of coffee and read the paper from cover to cover, then you'd ring your flatmate, your boyfriend and your mother. As soon as it looked like any real work was looming, you'd 'accidentally' break the photocopier, then do up a countdown-to-payday chart?

Anyone? Anyone at all remember? Because I do.

I hear people complaining that there aren't enough hours

in the day to do all they need to do. And I agree that time behaves differently within the confines of a workplace, that it's not governed by the same laws as time in the rest of the universe. But a couple of years back when I worked in an office, my colleagues and I were fully convinced that time *slows down* in a workplace. We insisted to each other (and anyone else who'd listen) that if we looked at the office clock at twelve-thirty, we could wait a full half-hour before looking again only to find it was *still* twelve-thirty. We eagerly anticipated the day when some prominent mathematician would do a seminal paper on the syndrome, and *then* people would be sorry they'd laughed at us!

But it never happened. Out of nowhere we've been swamped with work and the whole time-mutation thing has been subverted.

Freelancing and being self-employed have contributed to the decline. There's nothing to stop anyone spending half the morning surreptitiously reading a novel in a desk-drawer, and jumping guiltily whenever anyone comes into the room, but when you're self-employed, this kind of carry-on is going to make you look like a bit of a gom.

Or when most of your take-home pay is in productivity bonus, there isn't the same appeal in telling your caller that your systems are down and that you'll call them back (and then not doing so, of course).

I also blame the electronic office. We've become so comfortable with e-mail that it's customary to send them even to people in the office right next to you. In the old days you'd get off your seat, walk the four yards and while away twenty pleasant minutes insisting that your colleague had INDEED been out on the sauce the night before, you could tell by the state of him, just look at his eyes . . . But it's just not the same with e-mail.

So, before the old ways are lost for ever, I'm going to go on record and share with you some of the best ways to Doss at Work.

I work from home now (which has its own misery. I spent days sneakily reading a novel in a drawer, until I copped on), but when I worked in an office, food was central to our distractions. The day usually kicked off with everyone relating what they'd had for dinner the night before. Then, discussions of what we'd have for our lunch began just as soon as we'd finished eating the sandwich we'd brought in for it (never later than eleven). The pros and cons of Marks & Spencer versus Burger King versus the funny Italian place on the corner were furiously debated. And no sooner was lunch out of the way than the exploration of what we'd have at three-thirty began. KitKats or Cornettos? Magnums or Mars Bars? One of the most coveted duties was going to the bank to collect petty cash. We used to fight over it like dogs with a bone, because on most days you'd briskly conclude your business in the bank in ten minutes, which left you free to wander around the shops at your leisure. Then an hour and a half later you'd finally arrive back at work – stashing your purchases with the receptionist to be retrieved later – and burst into the office in a lather of indignation. 'The *queues* at that bank. It's ridiculous. Simply RIDICULOUS.'

But when it came to *really* taking our mind off things, there was no greater joy than that of a fire drill. We were usually given warning that it was going to happen, so we'd spend most of the morning sitting at our cleared desks, our jackets and bags poised to go. Then the minute the clanging started, we were propelled from our seats and pushing and sniggering our way out the door. The idea was that we'd gather at a muster station for the fire monitor to check that we weren't trapped in the 'burning' building, but instead most people took advantage of the confusion and disappeared for a quick pint or legged it to Boots to try on nail varnish.

Nowadays, even if the fire was *real*, there'd be some poor schmuck on a short-term contract who'd insist on staying at his burning desk, trying to finish a report for the following morning's meeting.

Another great ploy, I hear, is the 'bomb scare'. This works best in a retail or catering environment. A customer leaves a package behind. Now, it's clear to you that it's their gym bag or that evening's tea, but you don't tell your boss that. Oh no! Instead you start making noises about 'suspicious packages' and not wanting to get too close to it. Next thing you know everyone's standing on the street for an indefinite time until you get the all clear.

Extreme weather conditions can be diverting. In the glorious summer of 1995, someone managed to unearth an obscure Health and Safety regulation that said if the temperature in the office rose above a certain level, we were allowed to go home. So one of us (me?) brought in a thermometer, which we held in a boiling kettle, then presented to our boss. 'See! One hundred degrees. We're off to Soho Square.'

Another few suggestions for getting through the day: try barricading yourself into a cubicle in the ladies' and pretending the bolt is stuck. You could get a good fifteen minutes to yourself before they send in a man with a screwdriver. Get bad period 'pains' three times a month. (For best results, ideally you need firstly to be a woman, and secondly to have an easily embarrassed male boss.) Do vulgar anagrams of the managing director's name – it's always uplifting. As is the birthday of a colleague, because even when you hate the person, you can kill at least half an hour standing around a cake and saying, 'So? Any nice presents?'

But take care – attempts to alleviate the tedium can backfire. Once, when we just couldn't bear any more of Tuesday, one of us clambered on a chair and fast forwarded the office clock. Delighted, everyone streamed out ten minutes early, which was great. Until the next morning, when we were all bollocked for being late. So remember, when you move the hands of the clock forward, *don't forget to change them back*.

So there you are, some nuggets from another age. Now it's time for me to surf the net . . . whoops, I mean, do some more work. I'm so EXTREMELY busy I'm hardly going to waste any time visiting my favourite websites, now am I?

I mean, would you . . . ?

First published in the *Sunday Times*, October 2000.

Catholicism: Cheaper than Prozac, But is it Good for You?

The Sunday Times *had done a survey of Irish thirty-year-olds, canvassing their opinions on everything from spirituality to recreational drugs. To accompany publication of the survey, they asked several thirty-somethings to write articles on the various subjects. Mine was on – no, not on recreational drugs. Do you mind! But on spirituality.*

*I*reland, at the close of the twentieth century, is straddling a spiritual fault-line. Spiritually speaking, we're two nations, and the split is almost entirely along age lines. Above a certain vintage – and it's hard to see exactly at what age the cut-off point is – devout Catholicism is still the name of the game. Below that the waters become muddied, and a trawl through several thirty-something acquaintances indicates that they have a smorgasbord of beliefs, where some of the more attractive superstitions and rituals of Catholicism are included – we're still big on white weddings. And some of the more onerous ones – like the ban on sex outside of marriage – have been jettisoned.

This is a relatively new situation. After all, seven out of eight thirty-year-olds were born Catholic, the 'special' position of the Catholic Church is enshrined in our constitution, and as recently as the mid-eighties Ireland functioned almost as a theocracy.

So why is 'holy Catholic' Ireland no longer so holy or Catholic? There are many reasons, among them the energetic foot-shooting the Church itself has been doing. Contemporaneously, Ireland has finally come of age as a nation. While we were a fledgling semi-state existing in the shadow of Britain, we needed to cling to whatever defined us as anything other than British. Catholicism was one of the cornerstones. But now we can be whatever we want, and it appears that what we want is to be secular. Up to a point.

Then there's the effect of US culture, insidious and subtle. It affects every area of our lives – from what we eat and wear to what we believe in. And we seem to have developed a fast-food attitude to God – we want instant gratification spirituality. In the old days, people used to take the longer view: life might currently be a vale of tears, but big-time reward was a-coming the minute you popped your clogs. But nowadays no one is interested, to quote thirty-one-year-old Jenny Butler, in 'that martyrdom stuff. I want to be happy *now*, not when I'm dead, and if the Catholic Church can't guarantee it, I'll find something that can.'

I tried to trace the line of belief through the life of an average thirty-something. Apparently support for God was at an all-time high when we were children. But as Owen, a twenty-nine-year-old civil servant, says, 'When you're a child you'll believe anything. Let's face it, I believed in Santy Claus and the tooth fairy too.'

Then came our teens, when we rebelled against everything our parents held dear. It was as automatic as breathing. We turned against their choice of wallpaper, their choice of friends, and while we were at it, their choice of religion. No thought went into it, it was just a knee-jerk reaction.

Moving on into our twenties, we think we're 'immortal and untouchable,' according to Patricia, a thirty-two-year-old call-centre manager. 'We don't need God.'

But by the time we hit our thirties, something changes. People often start feeling a little more fragile, a little less resilient, and many experience a catharsis or watershed. Which can manifest itself in a myriad ways – ending a long relationship, getting married, changing jobs, buying a house, hitting the bottle hard or stopping entirely – certainly there's some kind of shakedown and rearrangement of priorities. The reasons are many. Our parents are either dead or ageing. We've been shunted forward so that often there's no other generation between us and death. We have to be the grown-ups and it's an alarming realization.

The death of a loved one – usually a parent – often triggers a search for 'something else'. Patricia, the call-centre manager, said that when her mother died, 'I couldn't get my head around that she'd just disappeared. I felt she had to be somewhere.' So a long-dormant belief in the afterlife was resurrected to give comfort.

Or else we've had children. One couple I know lived together for years, got married in a civil ceremony on a boat in the Caribbean, and never put a foot in a church except on

Christmas Day. But now that their eldest child is approaching school-going age, they've started going to Mass *en famille*. 'Neither of us believes,' thirty-two-year-old Sinead explained. 'But I wanted to teach my little girl the difference between right and wrong.' Sheepishly she said, 'I don't think it does me any harm either. It's half an hour a week where I get a bit of peace and quiet. It gives me a chance to think.' Then she added, 'It's particularly good when I'm feeling down. Cheaper than Prozac!'

The one thing I've noticed about those neo-Catholics who have recommenced a flirtation with the Church is their *à la carte* approach. I know *nobody* in their thirties who is a fully paid-up card-carrying Catholic on the issue of contraception. Or on the sacredness of Sunday Mass – if someone has to miss it, it's no biggie to them.

However, not every thirty-something who has become aware of the spiritual vacuum in their lives re-embraces Catholicism. Joe Rehill, a thirty-year-old software writer, insists he doesn't want to be hidebound by the rigours of organized religion. Unless it's an exotic, glamorous one. Like Buddhism, for example. There's been a proliferation of alternative spirituality, especially in recent years. A quick survey of my friends and acquaintances indicated we have tried, variously: meditation, I-Ching, Ogham sticks, crystals, reiki, white magic spells, rebirthing, chakra unblocking and Feng Shui. 'And why not?' a woman who wished to remain anonymous said of Feng Shui. 'The idea that changing the layout of your flat will bring good things into your life is no less extraordinary than accepting a round wafer from a man in an embroidered white frock and expecting good things to happen.'

But the one factor that seems to mark all thirty-something approaches to spirituality is the what-have-you-done-for-me-lately attitude. We insist on utilitarianism – it has to enhance our lives in some manner and make us feel better. This is a wild reversal of how it used to be, when people loyally obeyed the dictates of the Church, no matter how unpleasant the consequences.

And indeed, I've discovered that even though thirty-year-olds are likely to have some interest in spirituality, it's certainly not the first port of call in the pursuit of happiness. Winning the lotto is still the favoured route to a blissful existence. We're also very exercised about our jobs, houses and house prices. As Aiden Baker, a thirty-one-year-old sales rep says, 'I haven't time to go to Mass on Sunday because I've to go and worship at the temple of DIY. Homebase is the new God.' He was only half joking.

But to paraphrase the Jesuit spiritual teacher Anthony de Mello, 'In a hypothetical situation, if I could promise you perfect happiness, would you take it? It would mean giving up everything – your job, your car, your house, all your possessions, you'd be living on the street, but you'd be bliss-fully, joyously content. How about it?' Anthony de Mello suspected that no one would want to take him up on it. And when I put it to the people I interviewed, they said, 'Give up *everything*? Even my house?' I pointed out that they'd be sublimely happy, that they wouldn't care that they possessed nothing, but they all looked uncomfortable and eventually confessed they'd rather stay as they were.

Admittedly I'm writing from an urban situation and popular opinion has it that people are more devout in rural Ireland. But it seems that in the pursuit of happiness, though spirituality matters to a lot of thirty-year-olds – even if it only plays a walk-on part in their lives – at the end of the day, their money is riding on other things.

First published in the *Sunday Times*, October 1999.

THAT'S ME AWAY!

Now and again I take time off from writing and go on holiday.

Beside the Seaside

Lahinch, County Clare – the scene of my summer holidays every year in the sixties and seventies. The run-up to it featured: a) unbearable anticipation, and b) running battles with my mother as she spent the week before departure washing, ironing and packing clothes and as fast as she was ironing them I was wearing them. Which isn't on. Everyone knows you can't wear your shiny, good holiday clothes until the whistle is blown to officially launch the holiday.

Then the appointed Saturday morning would roll around and we'd be off. A Morris Minor with five children, two adults and one roof-rack. Mam attired – no matter how fine the weather – in a red, plastic raincoat to guard her travelling rig-out from puke-stains (other people's, not her own).

Nowadays, people drive from Cork to Clare in a couple of hours, but back then journeys took longer. These were pre-radio, pre-tapedeck days and we had to make our own entertainment. No bother to us! The singing usually commenced before we were out of the drive – 'Rhinestone Cowboy', 'Two Little Boys' and 'The Men Behind the Wire'. Not knowing the words or the tune was luckily never regarded as any impediment to taking the floor.

Punctuating the singing were the usual questions: 'Are we there yet?' 'How long more?' 'Can I make my wees?' 'Can I make my wees again?' 'Would I be in trouble if I got sick on my clean dress?'

Once we were the far side of Limerick, excitement burgeoned, and built as the towns swept past – Clarecastle, Ennis, Inagh, until we reached the metropolis of Ennistymon. By then we'd be nearly uncontainable, leaning into the front seats to urge the car forward. Out past the church, up the road, down into a little dip, up again to the saddle factory, over the brow of the hill, and suddenly there it was – the Atlantic, winking and twinkling magically, a blinding, dazzling expanse of silver diamonds.

We'd park at the prom, and open the car door to be hit by the intoxicating, powerful smell of clean, salty air, our namby-pamby city lungs astonished by its freshness and purity. Then down the worn stone steps to the unfeasibly vast sweep of flat, clean, wheat-gold sand.

There was never a rainy day during any of those holidays, or so it seems. In my mind's eye the sun was always splitting the stones and the sky was an intense blue with cotton-wool-ball clouds. The only concession I'll make to any kind of less-than-perfect weather was that sometimes there was a stiff breeze, causing the khaki-green marram grass to bend and sway. The sea was a powerful blue and green animal, thundering in, each wave trying to be bigger than the last, then sucking back out again. The white foam creating ever-changing lacy patterns, which stretched and expanded, got washed away, only to reappear in a different form with the next wave.

Into the togs immediately. The year I was six I'd outgrown my yellow, ruched-cotton togs, so was decked out in a home-made, lime-green, towelling bikini. I thought I was *it*.

The daily drill was that Mam sat on the Foxford rug, undressing, drying and dressing again a conveyor-belt of children, while everyone else paddled, jumped waves, swam, built sandcastles, dug moats, found sticks of driftwood and wrote – as you do – insulting messages to each other in the sand, fished tiddlers out of rock pools into nylon nets (and then, not really knowing what to do with them, just spilled them back in again).

Dad taught me to swim the year of the green bikini. Persuading me to float on my back, to put my head back into the muffled, bubbly silence, to let the cold water fill my ears, to bob and shunt on the swell and retreat of the waves.

After every swim, to get warm again, we all had a race along the strand in our bare feet – beaches littered with broken glass or rusty cans were still far away in our future.

Then into O'Connors to spend our meagre holiday money, temptation at every turn. The ceiling was festooned with buckets, shovels, beachballs, rubber-rings and fishing nets in fluorescent pink and yellow, and the shelves were arrayed with a dazzling choice of Summer Specials. (*Jinty*, as I remember, was my reading matter of choice until I graduated to *Jackie*.)

But it was cones I couldn't resist – the hum of the machine, the louder rattle as Mr O'Connor lowered the throttle, the sight of the thick luminescent-white rope of ice-cream squeezing from the nozzle and winding around and around itself on the cone, pinnacling with a little kiss-curl where it broke away from the machine. The moment before I began to eat was almost a mystic one as I absorbed the smell of the wafer, the smooth perfect ripples of pristine ice-cream. And I prayed that one day, when I was big, I'd be able to afford a 99 *and* raspberry syrup.

Unlike the fleshpot of Kilkee further along the coast, Lahinch didn't have much in the way of what my father called 'merries' (he meant amusements). There was a 'big' wheel – even to my starstruck, credulous eyes I could see that it was fairly small – and a couple of weary-looking bumper cars that held no interest for me until my teens (when overnight, heat and the smell of grease and cordite suddenly seemed sexy).

Mostly, funds didn't run to 'merries'. But the year the ghost train appeared on the site of the defunct chair o'planes, I realized I'd be going without a cone or two. I was mad about things I'd read about in Enid Blyton books like mazes, haunted houses and, most of all, ghost trains. Too nervous to go on my own, I persuaded Mam to come with me.

Oddly enough, we were the only takers. I couldn't understand why. Surely anyone with an ounce of sense would be spending all their holiday money on it? Into a little cart yoke we sat, and the minute the boy pulled the lever to move us forward I saw him breaking into a run. We disappeared through one of the plastic-ribbon room-divider things they have in chippers. After a few seconds of meandering around in darkness something began to tickle me and my heart nearly stopped with fright. Then I felt the ghostly hands move over to my mother to tickle her also. 'Stop that this minute,' she ordered and gave something a resounding slap. 'Ouch. Sorry, missus,' the ghost said contritely, in a Clare accent. The rest of the ride passed with absolutely nothing happening. We trundled around the area of an average sitting-room in the pitch black with not even the sound of an unearthly cackle to put the fear of God in me. When we got out we saw the boy who operated it, sitting down, nursing his eye. Someone appeared to have given him a puck. And when we came back the next year the ghost train was gone.

First published in the *Irish Independent*, September 1998.

The Lucky Suitcase

*H*olidays from Hell? Don't talk to me. A couple of years ago, Himself and myself went on a last-minute thing to Greece. We hadn't a penny so we signed up for one of those cheapo jobs, where you don't know where you're going to be staying until you get there. 'What do we care if it's a kip?' we laughed to each other, clinking celebratory start-of-holiday glasses. 'So long as it's sunny, won't we be grand?'

The sting in the tail was the compulsory insurance which almost doubled the cost of the holiday and wiped out most of our spending money, but we took it on the chin.

We landed in glorious, afternoon heat and in jaunty, holiday mode proceeded to the carousel to reclaim our bags. Spirits were high as we waited. And waited. And waited . . . Spirits weren't so high then, especially not ours, as it became clear that everyone else from our flight was on the bus, and Himself's bag hadn't yet appeared on the carousel.

Far from being helpful, Warren, our cheeky cockney chappie rep, was in a panic because there were rumblings of a mutiny from our fellow-travellers. They were officially on their holidays, and were none too happy about sitting in a hot, stuffy bus waiting for someone else's bag when there was retsina to be drunk. Warren abandoned us to go and soothe them by standing at the front of the bus and telling patronizing stories about the locals and their produce. ('They call it wine, but I say it'll come in very handy if the bus ever runs out of petrol! Hahaha!')

Meanwhile, we had to go to a small, dark, stifling office, with constantly ringing phones, where sweating moustachioed officials in military-type uniforms shouted at each other in a foreign language I can only assume was Greek. They kept coming in, shouting, picking up a phone, shouting, sweating, shouting, glaring at us, shouting, leaving. Then coming back for a quick shout. For some reason it put me in mind of *Midnight Express*. The only attention we got was when they relieved us of our passports. Oddly enough, this did nothing to reassure me.

A long time later, after they'd taken the scantiest of details and had done nothing to convince us we'd ever see the bag again, we were free to go. We stood on the steps, gulping in clean, free air, our elation screeching to an abrupt halt when we saw the sea of furious faces on the bus glaring out the windows at us. Sheepish and apologetic, we clambered aboard and off we went.

Every time the bus stopped outside a hotel, I was all agog, wondering if this was the beautiful be-swimming-pooled palace where I would spend my holiday. It never was.

But things were looking good when our names were called. Though there was no sign of a pool, we were led to brilliant white pristine modern apartments – and past them . . . Eventually, the rep stopped at something that can only be described as an outhouse. It was dark, dingy and depressing, and the bathroom looked as if a colony of spiders lived there. 'Home sweet home, mate,' Warren guffawed, then legged it.

A quick scout round the village showed that the beach was a twenty-five-minute walk and that there were no restaurants other than a wealth of chip-butty outlets, run by formidable Yorkshire women. When I tentatively enquired if I might have some traditional Greek food, I was told, 'Eee, luv, no call for it 'ere. Folk won't eat it.'

That night, after our dinner of Lancashire hot pot, as we fell into our scuzzy bed, the music started. It transpired that our outhouse was right next to a disco bar, which really only got into its stride at about one in the morning. Fantastic if you're a party animal. Not so great if you're on your holiers with a view to a rest. We lay awake all night, hysterical from sleep deprivation, feeling our intestines spasm in rhythm with the bass line.

The following morning, we had no choice but to go to the hotel on the hill for the newcomers' meeting, to see if the bag had turned up, even though we wanted everyone to know that we would never normally go to a newcomers' meeting. I'd hate people to think I had any truck with 'Traditional Greek Evenings' or bingo nights.

Himself had no summer clothes to change into, and as he sweated up the hill in his jeans and sweatshirt, cheeky cockney chappie Warren passed on his bike. 'Warm enough for you, mate?' he roared and laughed so much he swerved and nearly fell into the ditch.

Of the bag there was no news. It had gone truly AWOL. What should we do? He couldn't go round in his jeans for the entire week.

'You'll 'afta buy stuff,' Warren suggested. 'Keep receipts, and claim it back on your insurance.'

Clammy dread flushed down my body as I thought of our lean bundle of travellers' cheques. There was no room for going over budget on this holiday.

'Do you . . . ?' I could barely bring myself to ask. 'Do you . . . you know, *advance* money for that kind of thing?'

'You're joking, intcha, luv?' Warren convulsed. 'What do you fink we are? Nat bleeding West?'

My credit card had no room on it – in other words, it was about two hundred quid over the official limit – but I'd cannily noticed that none of the stores in the town had electronic tills. Which meant I could buy clothes for Himself with my flexible friend, without my card being cut up in front of me. (Not the first time it would have happened, and doubtless not the last.) Of course, there'd be armed guards waiting to greet me and throw me in a debtors' prison on my return to Gatwick, but what could I do? Round the shops we went and bought him shorts, T-shirts, sunglasses, togs and everything the well-dressed man requires for a sun holiday. But we needn't have bothered. It began to rain.

Himself took it hard. 'I've been to Greece about twenty times,' he said tearfully. 'And it's never rained before.'

He gave me a funny look and I realized he was wondering if I was some sort of jinx. I began to worry that our relationship might not survive the holiday.

Apart from fleeting chip-butty forays, we spent four days trapped in the tellyless outhouse. The nights we passed sniping at each other, cotton wool in our ears as we went quietly mad from the music. The bag never turned up, and by the time we went home we'd cheered up at the thought of taking the insurance company to the cleaners and spending the proceeds on a weekend in Barcelona. 'They'll rue the day they ever stitched us up with the compulsory insurance,' we laughed, tentatively friends again.

As we got off the plane I had a quick look around for the posse of policemen and Alsatians waiting to arrest me after my credit-card frenzy. No sign. But our gaze was inexorably drawn to a pile of bags thrown up against a wall. There, in the thick of things, shimmering with a kind of dynamic stillness, was something we recognized. No, surely not! It couldn't be ... But it was. Our bag. Our bloody bag. The trip to Barcelona wobbled, wavered and melted.

Reluctantly, we approached the Prodigal-son luggage and pulled it from the pile. The stamps and labels all over it indicated that it had spent the week living it up in Montego Bay.

'Lucky bastard,' I said, with grudging admiration. 'Come on. Let's go home.'

First published in *Irish Tatler*, July 1998.

Aerodrama

*I*n the late sixties, when I was very young and living in Cork, there wasn't afternoon television or Nintendos or McDonald's. The shops shut resolutely at five o'clock on Saturday evening and remained that way until Monday morning. Which meant that of a Sunday we had to make our own entertainment. This usually involved a drive, but my father was a man of vision and our Sunday-afternoon, nuclear-family jaunt in the Morris Minor was no ordinary affair – my dad's idea of a really top-notch Sunday afternoon was to *drive out to Cork airport and look at the planes.*

In those far-off forgotten days, Cork wasn't the cosmopolitan metropolis that it is today, and had about three planes a week taking off from its airport. Nevertheless, I can still remember the breath-inhibiting excitement. The airport seemed a model of space-age modernity: all gleaming floors and high, echoey ceilings. I liked nothing better than standing at an enormous plate-glass window and looking out at a sleek, white, metal bird. I'd stare till I nearly went blind, trying to see through the little portholes, desperate for a gawk at the unbearably glamorous people within. Convinced that every man jack of them was carrying hard-shell vanity cases, wearing

Grace Kelly suits and pillbox hats, fur coats slung casually over their shoulders, quaffing champagne and having arch and witty conversations with their travelling companions.

'Will I ever go on a plane?' I plaintively asked my father.

'You will of course,' he promised. 'If you get your long division right.'

Like I said, a man of vision.

And, as it happens, he was bang on the money. I *did* get my long division right and, after a brief spell on the dole, then another brief spell waitressing, landed the job in London as an accounts clerk. Initially, any time I wanted to come home to Ireland, it was a boat-and-train job. Flying was so expensive, it was just out of the question. Then, in the late eighties, a couple of airlines started a price war and suddenly air travel became accessible to the likes of me.

But they say you should never meet your heroes. Because somewhere between the late sixties and the late eighties, flying lost its glamorous lustre and just became a stress-laden means of getting from A to B.

Nowadays my blood pressure rockets any time I've to fly somewhere and it starts at the check-in desk. Under normal circumstances it takes me thirty seconds to check in. I just hand over my ticket, rattle off, 'Yes, I packed it myself, no, it hasn't been left unattended, no, no one has asked me to carry anything for them in my baggage, apart from that nice man in the balaclava.' 'Window or aisle?' they ask me. 'I couldn't care less,' I reply. Then they hand over my boarding card and Bob is our respective uncles. But it's not so simple for the people I always end up queuing behind. No matter how hard I try, I invariably pick the wrong check-in desk. I see a neat little queue made up of a mild-looking woman and a couple of men travelling alone and I position myself behind them, shunning the queues spilling over with squabbling extended-family units. But, lo and behold, just as the mild-looking woman gets to the check-in desk, she is joined by the eighteen people she's travelling with, who've been hiding, just out of sight, until now. They're usually flying as far as New Zealand or Borneo and, as well as their forty-nine pieces of luggage, they also want to check in a set of golf-clubs, a pram, and six thirty-foot canoes. It takes *hours* to set up all the connecting flights – Dublin to London to Singapore to Auckland to Dunedin – the check-in person usually has to go away and consult with a colleague in a back office. And nothing fills me with as much dread as the sight of her clipclipping her way down the departures hall. Eventually she comes back, and it takes hours more to label their luggage, then everyone gets their boarding card and I'm frantic with relief. But just as I shuffle forward, one of them turns back and casually asks, 'Any chance of a vegan meal?' That usually starts an avalanche of special requests – extra leg-room, a sodium-free dinner, a tour of the cockpit – and these things take time to sort out. Meanwhile, I seethe and fret behind them, convinced I'm going to miss the plane.

Not that I need worry. The flights I'm booked on are, without exception, delayed. But at least I now understand the double-speak on airport departure boards and can have a nice time idling around the duty-free (what's left of it). When 'GO TO GATE 23' flashes, it means 'The plane you'll eventually be getting on has just left Dublin and is on its way to London. Where it'll turn around and come back to Dublin and then you can get on.' 'NOW BOARDING' means 'Your plane has just left London and is on its way back to Dublin.' 'LAST CALL' means 'Your plane has just landed in Dublin and we'll be ready for boarding in about fifteen minutes.' 'FLIGHT CLOSED' means 'Now boarding.' 'FLIGHT DEPARTED' means 'Come on! Hurry! If you run, we'll let you on.'

Eventually, the glorious time for boarding rolls around. I march joyously down the metal corridor, waving my boarding card, then come screeching to a halt as a businessman in the first row stands in the aisle and ponderously arranges his possessions. First he takes off his jacket, folds it neatly, smooths it flat, then places it in the overhead bin. I can feel the queue building up behind me, streeling all the way back up the metal corridor. Then he takes his briefcase, opens it, takes some papers out of it, places the papers on his seat, spends a moment staring thoughtfully at nothing in particular, then slowly moves to put the case in the overhead bin. By this time the queue is stretching way beyond the gate, down past Bewleys and out into the duty-free. With tortuous caution he carefully places the case on top of his jacket and looks as though he might sit down and let me and the rest of the plane past him. The relief is enormous, but, no! Wait! He's forgotten he needs a pen from his jacket pocket! Out comes the briefcase and down comes the jacket. He fiddles around in the pockets until he eventually finds what he's looking for, then the whole folding scenario begins afresh. At this stage, the queue has snaked out of the duty-free, past the electronic, bag-checking yokie, into the departures area and on out into the car-park. I'm told it was tough travelling on the coffin ships, but at times like this, I feel I'd rather take my chances!

First published in *Irish Tatler*, September 1999.

'Nam Flashbacks

I'd never been to Vietnam before, but as the plane circled over dense foliage, emerald-bright paddy fields, graceful palm trees, their blades silver in the sunlight, and patient-faced, sloe-eyed girls working in the fields, I had a powerful sense of recognition. All that was missing was a chopper hovering overhead in the hard, blue sky and half a dozen green berets, climbing down a rope and up to no good.

It's impossible to avoid the war in Vietnam. No sooner had we landed in Ho Chi Minh than a commotion broke out in the seats behind us: a gang of fatigue-clad Australian lads doing their *Apocalypse Now*-revisited tour were getting very excited about the enormous anti-aircraft guns alongside the runway. There was much shouting about 'Gooks', 'The horror' and 'Tour of dooty'. And great was their disappointment when they saw steps being wheeled towards the plane – they'd hoped that they'd be allowed to disembark by abseiling down a rope instead.

And so to passport control. I've never encountered bureaucracy like Vietnamese bureaucracy. Even before we'd left Ireland we'd had to fill in a million forms, then a million more on the plane, and our first glimpse of Ho Chi Minh's immigration wasn't exactly encouraging. What looked like a twelve-year-old boy dressed up in his dad's army uniform was processing us. His hat was jammed low over his eyes – or maybe it was just miles too big for him. Either way, he cut a strangely intimidating figure.

The heat was indescribable as, with tortuous slowness, he worked his way through the queue. Suddenly he jerked his head up from his desk and directed a stream of high-pitched, screechy invective at us. We all made What-the-? faces at each other. Then the brat started semaphoring narrowness with his hands and suddenly we understood – the queue was getting too messy for his liking. Shuffling so that we were standing neatly behind each other – even the Aussie lads in their fatigues and buzz-cuts did as they were told – we muttered under our breaths, *very* under our breaths, about how a little bit of power was a dangerous thing.

Finally it was my turn and I staggered to the counter, buckling under the weight of my documentation. Sullenly, me laddo flicked through several of the forms, without paying them much heed. Then, without any warning, he screamed, '*Whe'e you stay? Whe'e you stay?*' I felt like directing his attention to the hundred or so forms in front of him, and saying that if he bothered his arse looking at any of them he'd find the name and address of my hotel on just about every page. Then I took a look at the machine-gun which hung off his arm and meekly recited the whereabouts of my hotel. He glared at me from beneath the peak of his hat, then stamped something on a bit of paper – I was in!

And I have to say he was the first and last unpleasant person I met in Vietnam.

A short half-hour later and Himself was also in. We traipsed out to where the humidity hit us like a flying brick. And the people! I'd never seen so many. *Ever*. Bangkok, where we'd just come from, was as empty as Connemara by comparison.

We eventually found our guide, an earnest young man called Binh, who directed us to a white Hiace van. And then began the journey from hell. Nobody paid any attention to what side of the road they drove on, they just pleased themselves, and a sea of motorbikes flew at us, swerving out of the way only at the last second. It felt like a particularly dangerous game of Space Invaders and was almost enough to distract me from my first impressions of Ho Chi Minh – which were of low-rise, shabby, faded French grace married to overcrowded, Asian pragmatism; crumbling villas with wrought-iron balconies housing ten times as many people as they had in colonial times; street names a strange hybrid of Vietnamese and French; baroque municipal buildings that wouldn't be out of place in Paris; occasional seventies, Soviet-style monuments, their greys and browns a brutal contrast to the ice-cream pastels of the French architecture. There were no skyscrapers, no silver towers reaching for the blue, nothing modern. Everything appeared old, down-at-heel, neglected. The pavements were like dotted lines, disappearing and lapsing into mud, then reappearing.

The ground floors of some of the French villas had been turned into shops, but without recourse to strip lighting or perky displays. They looked more like something you might come across in the Wild West, selling big sacks of loose produce – rice, maybe? Or grains? On the streets, stalls sold manky-looking fruit, misshapen and peculiar the way organic stuff is – though I suspected that the last thing it was in this casualty of chemical warfare was organic. Suddenly I felt a long, long way from Marks & Spencer.

And yet ... our hotel was beautiful. The guidebook had warned that rats were not out of the question in Vietnamese hotel rooms, which had made me want to cancel the trip altogether. But this was a modern hotel lobby – all pale, curving wood and smart, uniformed receptionists – which wouldn't have been out of place in London or New York. Maybe, for an authentic 'nam experience, I should have plumped for the rats and not this Western luxury, but feck it. You can only do what you can do.

We proceeded to reception – and then something happened which was to repeat itself again and again during my time in Vietnam. The girl checking us in looked up from her computer, clocked me for the first time and immediately choked with involuntary laughter. She got it together fairly quickly but for the rest of the procedure avoided looking at me, even while handing over my room key, and all the time her mouth twitched with barely contained laughter.

Fair enough. Whatever floats your boat, I thought,.

anxiously making for the lift and trying to ignore the silent convulsions of the liftman.

Our room was on the sixth floor, high enough to be able to spot the oily brown waters of the Saigon River in the distance. We flung our bags on the bed and straight away went out on to the humid streets, which teemed with people. Official estimates put the city's population at four million. Unofficially it's seven million. And even at first glance an astonishing number seemed to be amputees.

As we strolled around, every step that we took was followed by high-pitched, girlish hee-hee-hees (even from the men). They were so open about it and were clearly so amused that it was impossible to be offended.

Though there are almost no cars in Saigon, there are plenty of cyclos and literally thousands of motorbikes – all weighed low with people. On one I counted five people – Mum, Dad and three gorgeous children. And wouldn't you think that if there were only motorbikes and cyclos, it would be easy to cross the roads? But it was impossible – especially because no one paid the traffic lights any heed. Anxiously we stood as the lights changed from red to green back to red again and motorbikes continued to whip past us, covering us with dust. Enlightenment came in the form of a tiny woman, about four foot high and three stone, bearing several times her body weight in the two baskets swinging from her shoulder bar. Before our astonished eyes she stepped out into the dusty road in her shin-length pants, bare feet and coolie hat and didn't look right or left. The motorbikes roared and swerved easily around her and, without breaking pace in any way, she continued her serene journey to the other side.

We nodded knowingly at each other. So that's how you do it.

That night, we sat in the hotel's roof-top bar and looked over the city, and it took a moment to figure out what was wrong with the skyline – no neon, no advertising. There were lights from houses, but otherwise a peculiar absence of colour that seemed almost unnatural.

An early start the following day, as we drove out to the countryside to see the Cu-chi tunnels. Beneath a pretty forest, these are a vast network (250 km) of underground tunnels and chambers from which the Vietcong conducted their guerrilla war against the Americans. They had everything the well-equipped guerrilla outfit might need: sleeping quarters, a restaurant, even – God help us – an operating theatre. A tiny, insanely cheerful man showed us around with gusto, leaping in and out of hidden entrances and dragging us below ground to point out the hideous traps that awaited the US soldiers.

'When GI Joe hear he coming to Cu-chi, he know he will never be going home!' he grinned.

Standing in the sun-dappled glade, I stared at the man – his wiriness, his incongruous strength and his defiant cheeriness – and I suddenly understood why the Americans, for all their superior fire-power, hadn't had a prayer.

It was a horrible conflict, and Vietnam suffered appallingly, but my heart went out to the American soldiers – teenage conscripts for the most part – who were sent to fight this unwinnable war.

I was exhausted after the tunnels and I wanted to go back to the hotel and sleep and forget, for a while, about man's inhumanity to man, but Binh was all for bringing us to the war museum.

'There are some very good photographs,' he tempted, 'of deformed babies. Their mothers were bombed with agent orange.'

'Ah no, thanks.'

'They are really excellent,' he insisted.

'No!'

Disappointed and sulky, he took us back to the city in silence.

Just before we got out of the van, I turned to Binh and asked him why everyone kept laughing at me.

'They say you are like a doll,' he said – perhaps over-diplomatically. 'They are calling you Barbie.' Hmmmm. Then he added, 'They say your eyes are very round.' Now we were getting to the truth of the matter. 'And,' he went on, 'your nose is pointy.'

'And me?' Himself asked.

'They say you are like Licha'd Ge'e.'

'Richard Gere? Well, that's pretty good.'

That night we took our courage in our hands and decided to have dinner at one of the many outdoor food stalls. We chose one of the more high-rent establishments – as evidenced by miniature white plastic chairs scattered around the stand: Himself's knees ended up at around the same level as his ears and my bum got so wedged that when I stood up the chair came with me. The food was lovely, though.

The following morning I woke up early and decided to get my hair done – the way you do. Well, the humidity was playing havoc with my frizz and I'd had a successful blow-dry in Bangkok and I'd made the mistake of thinking that just because the two cities were only a couple of hours apart, they were similar . . .

'I'm off to get my hair done,' I told Himself, who replied, 'Fine,' mostly because he was still asleep.

It was only eight-thirty but already it was so hot and humid it was like breathing soup. I made my way along the broken-down pavement to where I'd remembered seeing a hair salon the previous day. The road was lined with stationary cyclos, with piles of bodies asleep in them.

No sooner was I through the door of the hairdresser's than the two women working there doubled over in hysterics. Old pointy nose strikes again. Once they'd recovered themselves they were charm itself and bombarded me with questions: Why was I in Vietnam? Who was I with? Did I like it?

Eventually they began washing my hair – with bottles of water. They were running a hairdresser's salon *and they had no running water*. Immediately I thought of the men asleep in their cyclos. When did *they* get to wash themselves?

Meanwhile, back at the hotel Himself was now fully awake and not at all happy. Thoughts – probably entirely unfounded – of me being kidnapped and sold into white slavery propelled him, in a bit of a panic, on to the streets. Just in time for the cyclo men to wake up and begin trying to sell him things. When he tried to explain that he didn't want to buy anything, that he was looking for someone, an amputee asked who.

'A woman,' Himself said, about to describe me.

'A woman!' the amputee said joyously, grabbing him with his good arm (well, his only arm). 'M'sieur, come with me, I can get you a woman.'

'No, I'm looking for my wife!'

'A wife! Yes, m'sieur, we can get you a wife.'

When I finally got back to the room, Himself was in a right fouler. 'I was worried sick about you and I nearly had to marry someone else!'

Well, after all that hullabaloo, there was nothing for it but to go shopping. But we were a long way from a Karen Millen. Instead we went to the market, an enormous indoor affair that sells everything from desiccated snake to exquisite, hand-painted lacquery. The heat, the noise and the smells were so intense I actually thought I might faint. And then something happened that can only be described as serendipity: right next to the dried monkey penises, I stumbled across a stall selling shoes. Now, in the normal run of things, I am becursed with strange, stunted feet, so that I find it almost impossible to get shoes small enough to fit me. But because Asian feet are smaller, there were tons of beautiful shoes *all in my size*. I was in shoe heaven.

Previously unpublished.

Read on for an exclusive taste of

ANGELS

The captivating new novel from
Marian Keyes

Published by Michael Joseph
in September 2002
at £16.99

1

I'd always lived a fairly blameless life. Up until the day I left my husband and then ran away to Hollywood, I'd hardly ever put a foot wrong. Not one that many people knew about, anyway. So when, out of the blue, everything just disintegrated like wet paper, I couldn't shake a wormy suspicion that this was long overdue. All that clean living simply isn't natural.

Of course, I didn't just wake up one morning and skip the country, leaving my poor sleepy fool of a husband wondering what that envelope on his pillow was. I'm making it sound much more dramatic than it actually was, which is strange because I never used to have a penchant for dramatics. Or a penchant for words like 'penchant', for that matter. But ever since the business with the rabbits, and possibly even before that, things with Garv had been uncomfortable and weird. Then we'd suffered a couple of what we chose to call 'setbacks'. But instead of making our marriage stronger – as always seemed to happen to the other luckier setback souls who popped up in my mother's women's magazines – our particular brand of setbacks did exactly what it said on the tin. They set us back. They wedged themselves between myself and Garv and alien-ated us from one another. Though he never said anything, I knew Garv blamed me.

And that was OK, because I blamed me too.

*

His name is actually Paul Garvan, but when I first got to know him we were both teenagers and nobody called anybody by their proper names. 'Micko' and 'Macker' and 'Toolser' and 'You Big Gobshite' were some of the things our peers were known as. He was Garv, it's all I've ever known him as, and I only call him Paul when I'm extremely pissed off with him.

Likewise, my name is Margaret but he calls me Maggie, except when I borrow his car and scrape the side against the pillar in the multi-storey car park (something that occurs more regularly than you might think).

I was twenty-four and he was twenty-five when we got married. He'd been my first boyfriend, as my poor mother never tires of telling people. She reckons it demonstrates what a nice girl I was, who never did any of that nasty sleeping-around business. (The only one of her five daughters who didn't, who could blame her for parading my suspected virtue?) But what she conveniently omits to mention when she's making her proud boast is that Garv might have been my first boyfriend, but he wasn't my only one.

However.

We'd been married for nine years and it would be hard to say exactly when I'd started to fantasize about it ending. Not, let me tell you, because I wanted it to be over. But because I thought that if I imagined the worst possible scenario, it would somehow be insurance against it actually happening. However, instead of insuring against it, it conjured the whole bloody thing into existence. Which just goes to show.

The end came with surprising suddenness. One minute my marriage was a going concern – even if I was doing strange stuff like drinking my contact lenses – the next minute it was entirely finito. Which caught me badly on the hop, as I'd always thought there was a regulation period of crockery-throwing and name-calling before the white flag could be waved. But everything caved in without a single cross word being exchanged, and I simply wasn't prepared for it.

God knows, I *should* have been. A few nights previously I'd woken in the darkness for a good worry. Something I often did, usually fretting about work and money. You know, the usual. Having too much of one and not enough of the other. But recently – probably longer than recently, actually – I'd been worrying about me and Garv instead. Would things ever get better? Were they better already and I just wasn't seeing it?

Most nights I didn't come to any conclusions and lapsed back into an unreassured sleep. But this time I was afflicted with sudden, unwelcome x-ray vision. I could see straight through the padding of the daily routine, the private language and the shared past, right into the heart of me and Garv, into all that had happened over the last while. Everything was stripped away and I had a horrible, too-clear thought: *We're in big trouble here.*

It literally made me cold. All the little hairs on my skin lifted and a chill settled somewhere between my ribs. Terrified, I tried to cheer myself up by having a little fret about the amount of work I'd have to do the following day, but no dice. So then I reminded myself that my parents were getting older and that I'd be the one who'd end up having to take care of them, and tried to scare myself with that instead.

After a while I went back to sleep, scratched my right arm raw, ground my teeth with gusto, awoke to the familiar sensation of a mouth coated with bits of grit, and carried on as normal.

I was to remember that *We're in big trouble here* when it transpired that we actually were. On the evening in question

275

we were meant to be going out for dinner with Elaine and Liam, friends of Garv's. And who knows, if Liam's new flatscreen television hadn't fallen off the wall and on to his foot, breaking his big toe in the process, so that I'd gone out instead of going home, maybe Garv and I would never have split up.

The irony is, I was *praying* that Elaine and Liam would cancel. The chances were good – the last three times we were supposed to meet up, it hadn't happened. The first time, Garv and I had bowed out because we were getting our new kitchen table delivered. (No, of course it didn't come.) The next time, Elaine – who's some bigwig in pensions – had to drive to Sligo to make a load of people redundant. ('The new Jag arrived just in time!') Then the last time I'd managed to come up with some spurious excuse which Garv had agreed with all too readily. This time it was their call.

Not that I didn't like them. Well, actually I didn't. Like I said, she's a bigwig in pensions and he's a stockbroker. They're good-looking, earn *tons* of money and are unkind to waiters. They're the sort of people who always seem to be getting new cars and going on holiday.

Most of Garv's mates were lovely, but Liam was a glaring exception: the problem was that Garv was one of those types who went around seeing the good in people – most people, anyway. This is a great quality in theory, and I'd no objection to him seeing the good in people I liked myself, but it was a bit of a pain when he persisted with the ones I didn't. Himself and Liam had been friends since junior school, in the days when Liam had been a lot nicer, and, even though Garv had tried very hard for my sake, he'd been unable to shake his residual affection for him.

But even Garv agreed that Elaine was terrifying. Shespokerealfast. Firingquestionsfromamachinemouth. How'swork? Whenareyougettinglisted? Her dynamic glamour reduced me to stammering inadequacy, and by the time I'd cobbled together an answer, she'd have lost interest and moved on.

But even if I had liked Liam and Elaine, I still wouldn't have wanted to go out that particular night – putting on a big, fat, happy head is that much harder if you've an audience. Also there was a pile of scary manila envelopes to be dealt with at home. (Plus two soaps eager to tend to my needs and a couch that couldn't do enough for me.) Time was too precious to waste an entire evening out enjoying myself.

And I was *so* tired. My work – like most people's, I would imagine – was very demanding. I guess the clue is in the name: 'work'. Otherwise they might call it 'flat on your back on a sunlounger' or 'having a deep-tissue massage'. I worked in a legal firm which had a lot of dealings with the US. Specifically, entertainment law. (After we'd got married, Garv, on account of his general fabulousness, had been seconded for five years to his company's Chicago office. I'd worked for one of the big legal firms there, so when we returned to Ireland three years ago I claimed to be well versed in US entertainment law. The kicker was that even though I'd done night classes and got some qualifications in Chicago, I wasn't a proper lawyer. Which meant I got tons of the work, most of the abuse, but only a fraction of the moola. I was more of an interpreter, I suppose; a clause which meant one thing in Ireland could mean something different in the States, so I translated US contracts into Irish law and drafted contracts that should – hopefully – stand in both jurisdictions.)

I lived in vague but constant fear. Sometimes I had dreams where I'd left out a vital clause and my firm got sued for four trillion dollars, which they deducted from my wages at the rate of seven pounds fifty a week, and I had to work there for all eternity paying it back. Sometimes, in those dreams all my teeth fell out as well. Other times, I'm sitting in the office and I look down to find that I'm naked and that I need to get up and use the photocopier.

Anyway, the day the balloon went up, I was very busy. So busy that my new fitness regime had gone by the board. I'd recently realized that biting my nails was the only exercise I was getting so I'd hatched a cunning plan – rather than ring Sandra, my assistant, to come and collect my dictaphone tapes, I'd walk the twenty yards to her office and hand-deliver them instead. But no time for such self-indulgence that particular day. A deal with a film studio was about to fall apart: if the contract wasn't finalized that week, the actor who'd attached himself to the project was going to walk.

For a minute there my job sounded glamorous. Take my word for it, it was as glamorous as a cold sore. Even the business lunches I occasionally had to go to at expensive restaurants weren't all that. You could never truly relax – people always asked a question requiring a long and detailed answer just after I'd put a forkful of food into my mouth, and whenever I laughed I was haunted by an irresistible fear that I had green food stuck in my teeth.

Anyway, the scriptwriter – my client – was desperate to get the contract all sorted out so that he could get his fee and his family could eat. (And so his father might finally be proud of him, but I digress.) The US lawyers had come to work at three in the morning, their time, in order to try and close the deal, and all day e-mails and phone calls zipped back and forth. Late in the day we dotted the final 'i' and crossed the final 't', and even though I was wrecked I felt light and happy.

Then I remembered that we were supposed to be going out with Liam and Elaine and a cloud passed over the sun. It wasn't so bad, I consoled myself; at least I'd get a nice dinner out of it – they were fond of fancy-dan restaurants. But God, I was exhausted. If only it was *our* turn to cancel!

And then, just when it seemed that we were beyond all hope, the call came.

'Liam's broken his toe,' Garv said. 'His new flatscreen telly fell on it.' (Liam and Elaine had every consumer durable known to man – and I stress *man*, not woman. Give me a mobile phone and a hair-curler and I'm happy. But Garv, being a man, yearned after digital this and Bang & Olufsen that.) 'So tonight's off.'

'Great!' I exclaimed. Then I remembered myself; they were his friends. 'Well, not great for him and his toe, but I've had a tough day and –'

'It's OK,' Garv said. 'I didn't want to go either. I was just about to ring them and pretend our house had been burnt down or something.'

'Dandy. Well, see you back at the ranch.'

'What'll we do about food? Will I pick up something?'

'No, you did it last night. I'll do it.'

I had just launched into an orgy of switching stuff off when someone said, 'Going home, Maggie?' It was my boss, Frances, and her *already?* might have been silent but I still heard it.

'That's right.' Lest there be any confusion. 'Going home.' Polite but firm. Trying to keep my prone-to-quaver-under-pressure voice free of tell-tale traces of fear.

'That contract ready for tomorrow morning's meeting?'

'Yes,' I said. No, actually it wasn't. She was talking about a different contract, one I hadn't even started on. There was no point whinging to Frances that all day I'd been frantically sewing up a great deal. She was an über-achiever, well on her way to being made a partner, and she'd made hard work into a performance art. She rarely left the office and popular opinion (not that she *was* popular, of course) had it that she slept under her desk and washed, like a bag lady, in the staff toilets.

'Can I take a quick look?'

'It's not really laid out properly yet,' I said awkwardly. 'I'd rather wait until it's all done before I show you.'

She gave me a watchful, too-long look. 'Make sure it's on my desk by nine-thirty.'

'Right!' But the good spirits engendered by being let off the hook for the evening had all leached away. As she hammered her heels back to her office, I looked appraisingly at the computer I'd just switched off. Should I stay and do a couple of hours on it there and then? But I couldn't. I was all out. Of enthusiasm, of work-ethic, whatever. Instead I'd get up very early and come in and do it then.

I hadn't eaten much all day. At lunch-time, instead of stopping work, I'd foraged in my desk drawer for a half-eaten Mars bar that I'd vaguely remembered abandoning some days earlier. To my delight, I found it. I dashed off the paper clips and the worst of the fluff and, I must say, it was delicious.

So as I drove home I was hungry, and I knew there would be shag-all in the house. Food was a big problem for Garv and me. We subsisted, like most people we knew, on microwaved stuff, takeaways and meals out. Now and again – at least, before things had gone weird on us – when we'd cleared our backlog of ordinary worries, we'd spend a bit of time worrying that we weren't getting enough vitamins. So we'd vow to embrace a new, healthier way and buy a jar of multivitamins, which we'd take for a day or so, then forget about. Or else we'd go on a mad splurge in the supermarket, pulling our arms out of their scurvied sockets lugging home heads of broccoli, suspiciously orange carrots and enough apples to feed a family of eight for a week.

'Our health is our wealth,' we'd say, pleased as punch, because it seemed that *buying* raw foodstuffs was an effective thing to do in itself. It was only when it became clear that the food had to be eaten that the trouble would begin.

Immediately events would set about conspiring to thwart our cooking plans: we'd have to work late or go out for someone's birthday. The ensuing week was usually spent in edgy awareness of all the fresh fruit and vegetables clamouring for our attention. We could hardly bear to go into the kitchen. Visions of cauliflowers and grapes constantly hovered on the corner of our consciousness, so that we were never truly at peace. Slowly, day by day, as the food went off, we'd furtively throw it out, never acknowledging to each other what we were doing. And only when the final kiwi fruit had been bounced off the inside of the bin did the black shadow lift and we could relax again.

Give me a frozen pizza any time, far less stressful.

Which is precisely what I bought for that evening's meal. I mounted the pavement, ran into the Spar and flung a couple of pizzas and some breakfast cereals into a basket. And then Fate intervened.

I can go without chocolate for weeks at a time. OK, days. But once I have a bit I want more, and the fluff-covered, lunch-time Mars bar had roused the hungry beast. So when I saw the boxes of handmade truffles in a chilled compartment I decided in a mad splurge of go-on-you-divil justification to buy myself one.

Who knows what would have happened if I hadn't? Did something as benign as a box of chocolates alter the entire course of my life?

Garv was already home and we greeted each other a little warily. We hadn't expected that this evening would be just the two of us; we'd been kind of depending on Liam and Elaine to dilute the funny atmosphere between us.

'You just missed Donna,' he said. 'She'll call you at work tomorrow.'

'So what's the latest?' Donna had a messy, high-concept love life and, as one of her best friends, it was my duty to provide advice. But she often consulted Garv to get what she called 'the male perspective', and he'd been so helpful that she'd rechristened him Doctor Love.

'Robbie wants her to stop shaving under her arms. Says he thinks it's sexy, but she's afraid she'll look like a gorilla.'

'So what did you advise?'

'That there's nothing wrong with women having hair –'

'Right on, sister.'

'– but that if she really doesn't want it, she should say that she'll stop shaving under her arms if he'll start wearing girls' knickers. Sauce for the goose and all that.'

'You're a genius, you really are.'

'Thanks.'

Garv pulled off his tie, flung it over the back of a chair, then raked his fingers through his hair, shaking away the vestiges of his work persona. For the office his hair was Ivy League neat:

shorn close at the neck and sleeked back off his face, but off-duty, it flopped down over his forehead.

There are some men who are so good-looking that meeting them is like being hit on the head with a mallet. Garv, however, isn't one of them; he's more the sort of man you could see day-in, day-out for twenty years, then just wake up one morning and think, 'God, he's nice, how come I never noticed him before now?'

His most obvious attraction was his height. But I was tall, too, so I'd never gone around saying, 'Ooh, look at how he towers over me!' All the same, I was able to wear heels with him, which I appreciated – my sister Claire had been married to a man who was the same height as her, so she'd had to wear flats in order that he wouldn't feel inadequate. And she really *loves* shoes. But then he had an affair and left her, so everything works out for the best in the end, I suppose.

'How was work?' Garv asked.

'Mostly awful. How was yours?'

'Bad for most of the day. I had a nice ten minutes between four-fifteen and four-twenty-five when I stood on the fire escape and pretended I still smoked.'

Garv works as an actuary, which makes him a cheap target for accusations of being boring – and on first meeting him you might confuse his quietness with dullness. But in my opinion it's a mistake to equate number-crunching with being boring; one of the most boring men I ever met was this gobshite novelist boyfriend of Donna's called John – you couldn't get more creative. We went out for dinner one night and he BORED us into the ground, loudly monologuing about other writers and what overpaid, meretricious bastards they were. Then he began questioning me about how I'd felt about something or other;

probing and delving with the intimacy of a gynaecologist. 'How did you feel? Sad? Can you be more specific? Heartbroken? Now we're getting someplace.' Then he hurried to the gents' and I just *knew* that he was writing everything I'd said into a notebook, to use in his novel.

'You're not to be jealous about Liam's flatscreen telly,' I said to Garv, happy to pretend that his subdued mood was down to his mate having more consumer durables than him. 'Didn't it attack him? It might have to be put down.'

'Ah,' Garv shrugged the way he always does when he's bothered, 'I'm not bothered.' (Though happy to discuss Donna's problems with her, you'll note his reluctance to talk about his own feelings, even when they're only about a telly.) 'But do you know how much it cost?' he blurted.

Of course I knew. Every time I went into town with Garv we had to call into the electrical department in Brown Thomas and stand before said telly, admiring it in all its twelve thousand pounds' worth of glory. Though Garv was well paid, he didn't earn anything like Liam's telephone-number wedge. And what with our high mortgage, the cost of running two cars, Garv's addiction to CDs and my addiction to face creams and hand-bags, funds just didn't run to flatscreen tellies.

'Cheer up, it probably broke when it fell off the wall. And one day soon you'll be able to afford one of your own.'

'Do you think?'

'Sure I do. As soon as we finish furnishing the house.' This seemed to do the trick. With a slight spring in his step, he helped unload the shopping. And that was when it happened.

He lifted out my box of go-on-you-divil truffles and exclaimed, 'Hey, look!' His eyes were a-sparkle. 'Those sweets again. Are they following us?'

I looked at him, looked at the box, then back at him. I hadn't a clue what he was on about.

'You *know*,' he insisted skittishly. 'The same ones we had when –'

He stopped abruptly and, my brow furrowed with curiosity, I stared at him. He stared back at me and, quite suddenly, several things occurred at once. The playful light in his eyes went out, to be replaced with an expression of fear. Horror, even. And before the thoughts had even formed themselves into any order in my consciousness, I *knew*. He was talking about someone else, an intimate moment shared with a woman other than me. And it had been recently.

I felt as if I was falling, that I would go on falling for ever. Then, abruptly, I made myself stop. And I knew something else: I couldn't do this. I couldn't bear to watch the downward spiral of my marriage begin to catch other people and spin them into the vortex too.

Shocked into stillness, our eyes locked, I silently beseeched him, desperate for him to say something to explain it, to make it all go away. But his face was frozen in horror – the same horror that I felt.

'I –' he managed, then faltered.

A sudden stab of agony shot up into my back tooth and, as though I was dreaming, I left the room.

Garv didn't follow me; he remained in the kitchen. I could hear no sound and I presumed he was still standing where I'd left him. This, in itself, seemed like an admission of guilt. Still in my waking nightmare, I was picking up the remote and switching on the telly. I was waiting to wake up.

By the same author

WATERMELON

On the day Claire gives birth to her first baby, her husband James tells her he's leaving her for another woman; a woman who doesn't even have the decency to be skinny!

So there's Claire, with a newborn baby, a broken heart, two extra stone and a birth canal ten times its normal size, with nowhere to go but home to Ireland. In the bosom of her family – her beautiful sister Helen, her soap-watching mother, her bewildered father – Claire starts to feel better. So when James slithers back into her life, he's got something of a surprise in store . . .

By the same author

LUCY SULLIVAN IS GETTING MARRIED

Clairvoyant Mrs Nolan tells Lucy Sullivan that she will be getting married before the leaves are on the ground a second time. When Lucy realizes that that means within the year, she is a little sceptical.

Staunchly denying the rumours of her impending nuptials firstly to her flatmates Karen and Charlotte, then to her friend Daniel, her brother and her difficult mother, Lucy is furious that she is the focus of so much gossip. For a start since she broke up with Stephen she doesn't even have a boyfriend. Well at least not yet . . .

RACHEL'S HOLIDAY

Here's Rachel Walsh, twenty-seven and the miserable owner of size 8 feet. She has regular congress with Luke Costello, a man who wears his leather trousers tight. And she's fond – some might say too fond – of recreational drugs.

Until she finds herself being frogmarched to the Cloisters – Dublin's answer to the Betty Ford Clinic. She's outraged. Surely she's not thin enough to be an addict? But still, it's about time she had a little holiday. What Rachel isn't expecting is middle-aged men in brown jumpers, and more group therapy than you can shake a stick at. Heartsick and Luke-sick, she seeks redemption in the shape of Chris, a man who might be more trouble than he's worth ...

LAST CHANCE SALOON

Tara, Katherine and Fintan have been best friends since they were teenagers in County Clare, in the days of leg warmers, pink stretch jeans and Duran Duran.

Now, in their early thirties, they live in London, where they are still bound together, but so far only Fintan has found true love. Tara is making do with the dreadful Thomas, who keeps his change in a little-old-ladies' purse, while Katherine's life is so orderly the only relationship she wants is with her remote control.

But when you're not up for change yourself, life sometimes has a way of making changes for you. And fate steps in to alter all their lives in wholly unexpected ways.